ADVANCE PRAISE

"Practical, inspiring advice for little entrepreneurs ready to think big."

—**Seth Godin,** author of *This is Marketing*

"A roadmap for every aspiring entrepreneur. This will drive you from thinking to doing."

—**Jason Feifer,** Editor in Chief of *Entrepreneur* magazine

"Brian shows how anyone can be successful in small business. Brilliant. Absolutely brilliant!"

—**Michael E.** Gerber, author of the E-Myth books

"Imagine having a business that gives you all the time, money, and freedom you ever wanted. Now imagine having a guide along the way. That's what Brian Scudamore's book can be for you!"

—**Joe Polish**, Founder of Genius Network

"If you want a bulletproof strategy for building a business from the ground up, Brian provides one of the best I've seen."

—**John Lee Dumas**, host of *Entrepreneurs on Fire* and author of *The Common Path to Uncommon Success*

"Pages jam-packed with helpful tips and stories that I wish I could've sponged up in my earlier founder days. Stories you'll wanna flag and come back to!"

—**Ryan Holmes**, Founder of Hootsuite and League of Innovators

"Brian is an entrepreneurial master. His book lays out the path for business success. Read it, act on it, and reap the rewards!"

—**Jack Daly**, serial entrepreneur, CEO coach, and world-renowned speaker and author

"*Brian shares his wisdom so anyone who wants to start a business can do it without the heartache but with all of the success. He is truly on a mission to empower others!*"

—**David Meltzer,** speaker, author, sports executive, investor, and entrepreneur

"*Brian helps people realize their dreams of business ownership through a proven formula.*"

—**Jim Treliving,** Chairman of Boston Pizza International and star of CBC's *Dragons' Den*

"*No one else on earth has done so much with a pile of junk, and now he's sharing his secrets on how you can do it too!*"

—**Randy Hetrick,** Founder of TRX/OutFit

"*A fantastic book full of genius ideas, great stories, and priceless wisdom from a world-class entrepreneur.*"

—**John Spence,** top business and leadership expert

"If you've ever had that itch to build a business, give this a read! You'll get a clearer picture of how to get started, pitfalls to avoid, and how to ultimately find your own success."

—**Brit Morin,** Founder of Offline Ventures and Brit + Co

"For anyone looking for a master class on how to take the leap and build something great, Brian's guide will help them navigate the journey."

—**Guy Raz,** Creator of *How I Built This* podcast

"Brian Scudamore is an expert at helping others find their entry point to entrepreneurship. He's done it all and believes anyone can find success as a business owner—they simply have to get started."

—**Jim Kwik,** *New York Times* bestselling author of *Limitless*

"A fast, inspiring read for people passionate about business ownership. You'll learn how to create a values-based business and gain professional success in ninety minutes. Highly recommend it!"

—**Chip Wilson,** Founder of lululemon

"One of the greatest parts of being an entrepreneur: you get to control your own destiny. One of the hardest parts of being an entrepreneur: there are many things you can't control. This is an ironclad playbook from a proven entrepreneur so you can go off and build a successful business around what you can control."

—**Alex Lieberman,** Co-Founder of Morning Brew

"From his humble beginnings to building a massive home services business, Brian understands the journey and has helped countless others realize their own dreams of entrepreneurship along the way."

—**Charles Chang,** President and Founder of Lyra Growth Partners Inc.

"In BYOB: Build Your Own Business, Be Your Own Boss, *Brian Scudamore challenges anyone with a dream of business ownership to dive in. By sharing a series of inspiring anecdotes from his thirty years in industry, advice from other successful entrepreneurs, and a concrete how-to plan, Brian has written a book that will help readers stop thinking and start doing."*

—**Verne Harnish,** Founder, CEO, and author of *Scaling Up (Rockefeller Habits 2.0)*

"Every entrepreneur makes mistakes. Brian Scudamore knows that more than anyone. Here, he uses his hard-won expertise to help aspiring and new business owners overcome their fears of failure, home in on their greatest strengths, and get on the fast track to success. This book is a great help!"

—Jack Stack, President and CEO of SRC Holdings Corp.

"Brian Scudamore has achieved a lot during his thirty years as an entrepreneur, including the launch of three hugely successful brands. Now he's dedicated to using his experience to help others achieve their dreams of business ownership."

—Gino Wickman, author of *Traction* and *Entrepreneurial Leap*

"As a serial entrepreneur and long-time observer of what works (and what doesn't!), Brian provides the tips, tactics, and strategies you need to launch a high-potential business."

—Ian Portsmouth, former publisher and editor for *Profit* magazine

"Brian Scudamore is one the great entrepreneurs of our time. His book provides readers with the tools, techniques, and acumen they need to hone the self-starter mindset required to achieve their dreams."

—**Josh Machiz,** Chief Digital Officer and Head of Client Engagement at Nasdaq

"Serial entrepreneur Brian Scudamore believes anyone can become a business owner and create a sense of freedom, community, and legacy—they just need focus, effort, and a little guidance. In this book, he shares the secrets to his success, an easy-to-follow plan, and inspiring stories of entrepreneurship."

—**Jordan Harbinger,** Creator of
The Jordan Harbinger Show

"An adventure through business that includes the secret sauce on how to grow and scale quickly. A must-read for anyone ready for the adventure of entrepreneurship."

—**Ryan Deiss,** Founder and CEO of Scalable.co and DigitalMarketer.com

"Brian Scudamore is the mentor I wish I had when I started my first business! He guides aspiring entrepreneurs so that they can understand the moving pieces of starting a business, and best of all, he does it with wit and wisdom! If you have been thinking about owning your own business, do not pass go until you read this book. You'll thank yourself later."

—Misty Lown, CEO of More Than Just Great Dancing!

"Brian Scudamore is a business maverick! His insatiable desire to study, learn, and master the art of execution and performance is world class. BYOB: Build Your Own Business, Be Your Own Boss *is the blueprint to help you understand what it takes to win in business and become an extraordinary example of what's possible."*

—Gary Mauris, CEO of The DLC Group

"If you want to be a successful business owner, listen to people who've done it already, like Brian. In this fantastic book, he outlines just about everything you need to know to get started, get customers, and get profitable."

—Tucker Max, four-time *New York Times* bestselling author

"I have gifted this book to every friend who has been stuck at what if. No more excuses after reading this book. Thank you, Brian, for the roadmap to my dreams!"

—**Andre Norman,** CEO of Academy of Hope

"Don't do entrepreneurship alone. Brian is the master at growing businesses, and this book is your perfect guide."

—**Mike Michalowicz,** author of *Get Different* and *Profit First*

"Read Brian's newest book. I've been a franchisee for three years, a franchisor with three companies, and an entrepreneur for seventeen years. I also worked alongside Brian as the first COO of 1-800-GOT-JUNK? for six and a half years. This book gives you rare real insights into both paths, which will help anyone on an entrepreneurial journey."

—**Cameron Herold,** Founder of the COO Alliance and author of *Vivid Vision*

"If you're looking to start a business but wondering how, this book will provide you with the confidence to get started and the map to guide you along the way. Starting a business is tough, but it is also very doable and very rewarding. Grab a copy and see for yourself!"

—**Nicholas Hutchison,** Founder of BookThinkers Inc.

"Brian Scudamore cares about entrepreneurs. He dropped out of school, went into the junk business full time to make nine figures, and now teaches ordinary people to start exceptional businesses themselves. When Brian puts out a new book, you should read it!"

—**Evan Carmichael,** Youtuber

"BYOB: Build Your Own Business, Be Your Own Boss is a guidepost for the next wave of business leaders and entrepreneurs. The amount of insight is off the charts. So many gold nuggets! So many ideas worth using on your own journey, especially if you're just starting out."

—**Adam Contos,** CEO of RE/MAX Holdings Inc. and author and host of the *Start with a Win* podcast

"Many people want to build a great business but end up sacrificing their personal lives and end up with regrets. What I respect most about Brian is how he has been able to achieve extraordinary professional success while prioritizing his personal life. If you want to thrive professionally and personally, Brian is a person worth learning from."

—**Geoff Woods,** Co-Founder and President of ProduKtive and author of *The ONE Thing*

"This is the book I needed when I was taking the leap to being a full-time entrepreneur. This book lays out a foundation for building a business from the ground up. If you're stuck in the what-if stage, get your hands on a copy of this."

—**Hala Taha,** CEO and Founder of YAP Media and host of *Young and Profiting* podcast

"Brian Scudamore is the ultimate CEO. He's built iconic businesses from the ground up by sharing his vision of the future and implementing simple systems with amazing people. His culture has become legendary, and his results are undeniable. BYOB: Build Your Own Business, Be Your Own Boss *Brian lays out the blueprint for how to do it and how anyone can build a business that stands out and stands the test of time."*

—**Jesse Cole,** owner of Savannah Bananas

BYOB

**BUILD YOUR OWN BUSINESS,
BE YOUR OWN BOSS**

BYOB

BUILD YOUR OWN BUSINESS, BE YOUR OWN BOSS

BRIAN SCUDAMORE

WITH ROY H. WILLIAMS

LIONCREST
PUBLISHING

BYOB

Build Your Own Business, Be Your Own Boss

ISBN   978-1-5445-2736-9   *Hardcover*

         978-1-5445-2734-5   *Paperback*

         978-1-5445-2735-2   *Ebook*

I would like to dedicate this book to my O2E Brands family, to the hundreds of franchise partners across 1-800-GOT-JUNK?, WOW 1 DAY PAINTING, and Shack Shine. Your endless passion, grit, and enthusiasm have turned O2E Brands into a globally recognized brand, where we turn ordinary services into exceptional experiences for our customers every single day. Thank you for believing in growing bigger and better, together. Here's to you!

CONTENTS

Psst...you'll see 》s throughout the book. If you are easily distracted and always in a rush like me, you can flip through, find a 》 and get the big takeaways.

INTRODUCTION

RSVP: ✔ YES!

I wrote this book to encourage you.

I often hear people refer to business ownership as "Living the American Dream." While *my* home is in Canada, I definitely feel like I am living the dream!

After thirty years in business, it's become crystal clear to me that I'm on a mission. A mission to inspire others to live the dream too, and to start, build, or be a part of the wonderful world of entrepreneurship.

Before you start this book, I need you to do something.

This book is called BYOB (because you're invited to join the party). It's a conversation, a sharing of lessons learned, a journey...best enjoyed with a beverage of your choice. So, go grab a beer, an iced latte, a fizzy drink. Whatever you'd have while chatting with a friend.

You've picked up this book and RSVP'd yes. I'm hoping it's because you have the same dream I did.

How you start your business doesn't matter. What matters is that you have a fire burning inside to **B**uild **Y**our **O**wn **B**usiness or to **B**e **Y**our **O**wn **B**oss. You just haven't taken the leap—yet.

I'd like to encourage you, give you a shot of confidence, and present you with two equally awesome choices for starting your own business. I want to give you a healthy little push :)

We have ninety minutes together.

Ready?

Let's do this!

Cheers,

Brian

1

VISION

WHEN YOU HAVE A VISION BURNING DEEP WITHIN YOU TO:

- invent an entirely new business model, or

- birth a business no one has ever seen, or

- create a category that has never existed

you'll need to start with a blank sheet of paper. By using the power of your vision and going into extreme detail, that blank piece of paper will become your Painted Picture—a crystal-clear snapshot of where you'll be in the future.

Your mind works consciously and unconsciously 24/7 to bring into reality the things you see in your imagination. You are limited only by the clarity of your vision.

It's almost as if, at the moment of commitment, the universe conspires to assist you.

Starting a business from a blank sheet of paper requires a high degree of creative vision and the financial and emotional staying power to survive the learning curve. The upside of the blank-sheet startup is that you get to say, "I did this, all alone, by myself."

Entrepreneurs like my friend Shaquille O'Neal don't feel the need to say, "I did this, all alone, by myself." Shaq didn't win four championship rings by inventing basketball. He won them by playing an already existing game in an exceptional way.

Shaq is a leader and a team builder who knows how to coach people to execute what they've been trained to do. He isn't looking for a blank sheet of paper. He's looking for a well-thought-out plan to execute with his team. That's why the franchise player became a franchise partner.

The Painted Picture of the future that Shaq sees in his mind is to provide good jobs to people who need them, and then to coach those people on how to turn every customer into a joyous brand ambassador.

When your company culture is all about happy people and happy customers, the money comes rolling in. Shaq has amassed a nine-figure fortune after becoming a franchise partner, but he doesn't make the exact dollar amount public, saying, "My mother would be disappointed if I talk about numbers."[1]

《 The first choice you, as an aspiring business owner, will need to make is whether

> 1. you will focus your vision on creating, testing, and refining something that has never previously existed, or

> 2. you will focus your vision on recruiting and coaching a team to help you execute a plan that has already been created, tested, and refined by someone else. 》

Although I've built my career on choice number one—starting from scratch—I often think that if I had found a franchise I believed in, I might have become a franchise

---

1 Abigail Gentrup, "Shaquille O'Neal's Long List of Business Investments," *Front Office Sports*, March 4, 2021.

partner rather than a franchisor. Most successful business owners choose choice number two—execute an already-proven plan.

In this book, I'm going to show you how to move forward with choice number one: how to create, test, and refine something that has never previously existed. And I'm going to tell you how to do number two: choose a franchisor who has successfully created a plan that has already been created, tested, and refined.

Regardless of which of these two options you choose, I'm going to make sure you understand what you need to know to choose your own adventure.

Ready. Set. Go!

2

PEOPLE

THE SIMPLEST DEFINITION OF A COMPANY'S BOOK VALUE is the net value of a firm's assets found on its balance sheet, roughly equal to the total amount all shareholders would get if they liquidated the company.

By this definition, the book value of the Orlando Magic in 1992, the Los Angeles Lakers in 1996, and the Miami Heat in 2004 was exactly the same the day *after* they signed Shaq as it was the day before. But due to the human capital those teams had acquired, each of them immediately became worth a lot more money when they had Shaq on their side.

《 Never underestimate the value of human capital. It will buy you what money cannot. 》

A bunch of kids on the playground decide to play a game. Two captains face the rest of the kids and take turns choosing who will be on their side. The game is won or lost when the teams are chosen.

Every business owner is a team captain. The number of points you score is largely determined by who you choose to be on your side.

If you become a franchise partner, your franchisor will be one of the players on your side. But regardless of whether you start a one-of-a-kind business or become a franchise partner with a winning franchise, don't make the mistake that I made when I started 1-800-GOT-JUNK?. Don't be the smartest person in the room.

I would have grown a lot more quickly if David Ogilvy had been my coach.

Ogilvy was a British advertising tycoon. Every time he opened a new office in one of the world's most important cities—132 in all—he would leave a set of wooden Russian nesting dolls on the branch manager's desk for them to find on their first day of work.

The manager would open each of those dolls of decreasing size, placed one inside another, until he or she finally came to the smallest one. Inside that tiniest doll would be a slip of paper, like you might find in a fortune cookie, with a quote from Ogilvy, saying, "If each of us hires people who are smaller than we are, we shall become a company of dwarfs. But if each of us hires people who are bigger than we are, we shall become a company of giants."

《 Your team is vitally important to your success. 》

My startup junk-hauling business, The Rubbish Boys, was pulling in about a million dollars a year when I found myself haunted by the questions, "What would things be like if I got the right people? How different would my business be?"

I had created my Painted Picture of happy, uniformed employees in clean, shiny trucks becoming the FedEx of junk removal, but we plateaued. I realized I'd hired the wrong people and needed to start again if I wanted to turn my vision into reality.

It broke my heart when I fired the whole company—all eleven people—in a single day. But I did it.

Then I created "The Beer and BBQ Test."

It's two simple (and delicious) steps to find people who truly fit our culture.

First I ask myself:

- Do I find this person interesting?

- Is this person genuinely interested in what we do?

- Do we share a common passion and goal in life?

- Is this person fun to talk to?

- Would I enjoy riding in the truck with them?

- Can I imagine myself having a beer with them?

The second part is about deciding if the person is a good addition to our team overall. If I threw that candidate into a group setting, like a company BBQ, would they find a way to connect? What do they bring to the group dynamic?

The Beer and BBQ Test helped me find the Dave Lodewyks, the Jason Smiths, and the Tyler Wrights of this world—people whose companionship I truly enjoyed. Hiring the right people revolutionized my business.

The Rubbish Boys quickly transformed from a bunch of guys who hauled junk to make money into a happy team of people championing a vision and a cause. We were in the business of making people happy!

"We make junk disappear. All you have to do is point."

Never underestimate the transformative power of human capital.

3

SYSTEMS

When I started The Rubbish Boys, I had to figure everything out the hard way: on my own.

Experience is the name we give our mistakes.

Niels Bohr, a scientist who won the Nobel Prize in Physics, said, "An expert is a person who has made all the mistakes that can be made in a very narrow field."

Based on that definition, I am definitely an expert. I've made every mistake that can be made at least once. A couple of the big ones I've made twice.

After I made the painful decision to fire all my employees and start my business all over again, it occurred to me that my only marketing plan had been to spray-paint my name on the side of my truck. I was secretly hoping that everyone in Vancouver would see it and say, "I keep seeing your truck everywhere!"

I didn't understand sales until I went knocking door-to-door saying, "Hi, I'm Brian from The Rubbish Boys and I see that you've got a pile of junk at the back. Can we take that away for you?"

I didn't understand customer service or public relations. And I didn't have a clue how to manage the finances. I quickly learned that just because I had checks in my checkbook didn't mean I had money in the bank!

> « It takes a lot of time and frustration to become an expert. But if you are willing to listen to an expert, they can help you become one faster and easier. »

If you're paying attention to the outcomes of your decisions, you can't make the same mistake twice. Because the second time you make it, it's not a mistake; it's a choice.

I had been in the junk-hauling business for about ten years when I finally began to ask the right questions. One of them was, "How do I organize this into a neat package?"

I was reading Michael Gerber's *The E-Myth* about Sarah's Pie Shop when I began to understand that your business has to have a **vision** that inspires your people and the public, skilled **technicians** to do the work, and a manager to make sure the **systems** are being followed.

Sarah was good at making pies. She was a skilled **technician**, but she had no **system**—no recipe—she could teach others.

Gerber called his book *The E-Myth* because skilled technicians often believe the entrepreneurial myth that their skill as a technician somehow qualifies them to fulfill the twin roles of:

1. visionary creator, and

2. manager of a systems-based business.

The visionary creator of a new business is like the builder of a race car.

Do you want to *build* a race car? Or do you want to *drive* a race car? Both paths can lead to great success, but winning the race is much more likely if your race car is already on the track.

The franchise partner is the one who drives the race car, wins the race, pops the cork on the champagne bottle, collects the trophy, and cashes the check.

Some people enjoy building race cars, but entrepreneurs like Shaq just want to drive a car that can win.

The race cars built by franchisors are the refined systems and solutions that allow franchise partners to go faster, achieve more, and get support when they break down. They use these systems and solutions to accelerate their speed, steer around obstacles, and fly across the finish line to a wildly waving checkered flag.

1. You cannot win without tested and refined **systems**. Create them or buy them.

2. You need **people** who believe what you believe and feel what you feel. Find them and hire them.

3. Your people will be energized and empowered when they embrace your contagious **vision.** ⟩⟩

You are their coach and manager.

And you own the race car.

4

MORE ABOUT SYSTEMS

No matter how many years you've been flying airplanes, you still go through that preflight checklist, step-by-step, before you lift that plane off the ground.

There are old pilots and there are bold pilots, but there are no old, bold pilots.

Startup entrepreneurs rarely take the time to experiment, refine, and systematize every little process. But you will never really accelerate your business until you have created that "preflight checklist" and an "in-flight checklist" for all of your people. They can't learn to fly without them.

You need systems and processes if you want your business to rise high.

The absence of refined systems and procedures was what limited Sarah's Pie Shop. If you want to see this firsthand, buy a cup of coffee from a one-of-a-kind coffee shop. That owner loves the coffee business. The staff is passionate about coffee, too, and the owner and the staff love their customers.

Sit in that coffee shop and count the total number of cups that are created and served in fifteen minutes.

Now walk into Starbucks and do the same thing. Notice the economy of motion and the fluidity of the staff. No matter which of the 32,938 Starbucks you walk into, and no matter which barista serves you, the coffee is always the same.

You might actually prefer that little one-of-a-kind coffee shop, but I'm pretty sure the average Starbucks is making a lot more money.

McDonald's doesn't serve the best hamburger you've ever had, but no matter which of the 39,198 worldwide McDonald's you walk into, a Big Mac with fries is always the same.

Replication, duplication, and consistency require systems and processes. When you have systems and processes, you make it easy for your people to operate at maximum efficiency, and you make it easy for your customers to buy from you. Your consistent performance will give your customers confidence that every interaction with you will always be the same.

Familiarity is a powerful thing.

5

COMPANY CULTURE

"There's no chance that the iPhone is going to get any significant market share. No chance."

—Steve Ballmer, Microsoft CEO, 2007

ON MAY 26, 2010, APPLE SURPASSED MICROSOFT TO become the world's most valuable technology company. In 2018, they became the world's first company to achieve a $1 trillion valuation. The keys to Apple's success were Vision-People-Systems, Culture-Story-Experience.

We're going to see the importance of these things again and again throughout this book.

The culture of Apple has always been intensely visionary: *innovate,* invent, *innovate,* invent, *innovate,* invent, *innovate,* invent.

Your culture is an expression of who you are—the final product of your vision, and the management choices you've made, including recruitment, training, and systems.

For ten years, Carl Schramm managed a $2 billion fund for stimulating visionary entrepreneurship in America. He's written countless business books about entrepreneurship, including *Burn the Business Plan.*

When Pulitzer-nominated reporter Dean Rotbart asked Schramm if getting an MBA was the ticket to becoming the visionary entrepreneur of a startup, Schramm literally laughed out loud as he said, "No."

Instead, Schramm said the three characteristics possessed by every successful entrepreneur who started with a blank sheet of paper are:

1. Determination. Keep failing forward.

2. Experimentation. Keep failing forward.

3. Innovation. When you finally figure it out, create a system.

It sounds like Schramm gave Rotbart the perfect description of how Steve Jobs built Apple, doesn't it?

6

UH-OH

Right now, three race cars I've built are being driven at high speeds by franchise partners worldwide: 1-800-GOT-JUNK?, WOW 1 DAY PAINTING, and Shack Shine.

But I've actually built four race cars...and the one and only time I skipped step two—experimentation—it crashed into the wall and I had to limp away.

My third brand, You Move Me, was launched in a fit of frustration when the moving company I hired arrived late, left muddy footprints on our carpet, destroyed our mattress, lost a bunch of our stuff, and broke my wife's favorite plant.

I said, "Someone needs to make the process of moving stress-free for the customer!" And then I decided that person should be me.

The little devil on my shoulder started whispering in my ear, "Sure, yeah, you can do this. It's just guys in trucks. You've done it in junk hauling. You've done it in house painting. You can do it in the moving space. Of course you can. You've got this."

The visual brand for You Move Me was amazing and our trucks were beautiful. Our Painted Picture of the future was to treat people like they were our friends on moving day. We brought them coffee in the morning because their coffee maker was all boxed up, right?

Our plan was to do exactly what a friend would do.

And at the end of the job, we'd give them a couple of housewarming gifts: a nice plant and a cheerful, smiley You Move Me mug including a card signed by each of the movers.

But those two little bookends were not enough to make us unique and special. Our plan was to revolutionize the moving industry, but our race car didn't have enough horsepower. The truth is that we were still trying to figure out the business.

We went straight from:

number 1: Determination,

to number 3: Innovation,

and left out number 2: Experimentation.

We failed to take the time to test and refine our assumptions.

I had convinced myself that I was an expert in businesses that involved technicians in trucks, but as it turned out, I wasn't finished making all the mistakes that could be made.

To make matters worse, I ignored the advice of a real expert, Dina Dwyer of the Dwyer Group, who has twenty-three different franchises.

I told Dina that I was going to launch You Move Me with twenty-five franchise partners, straight out of the gate.

"How are you going to do that?" she asked.

"Twenty-five of my most successful 1-800-GOT-JUNK? franchise partners are all wanting something more."

"Don't do it," she said. "They will turn their focus to the shiny new object and take people and energy away from 1-800-GOT-JUNK?."

But I did it anyway. I didn't bother with experimenting and refining the business at a small scale before I launched.

Of those twenty-five franchise partners, more than half threw in the towel within the first two years. It wasn't a pretty picture. It was only our history of 1-800-GOT-JUNK? success together that kept these franchise partners from being deeply and dangerously upset with me.

I'm proud we tried. I'm proud we were able to sell You Move Me so that the new franchisor could continue to develop the concept and make it even better. And I'm proud that our remaining franchise partners were taken care of and continued to stay in the business.

I called Dina and told her, "You were right."

7

COMPANY STORY

The *E-Myth* was about Sarah and Sarah's Pie Shop.

But the Sarah in *this* book is me, the college dropout who founded The Rubbish Boys while he was waiting in the drive-through line at McDonald's and saw a ratty old pickup with "Junk Hauling" spray-painted on the side with a phone number.

I said to myself, "I could do that."

I believed the only two things I needed were a beat-up old truck and a can of spray paint, so I bought an old Ford and a can of Krylon. Five minutes later, the side of my truck said "The Rubbish Boys" but most of the real estate on the side of the truck was the phone number, 738-JUNK.

It wasn't long before we became known as 738-JUNK. People saw and remembered that phone number but forgot our name.

Mike worked for The Rubbish Boys for several years. We spent a lot of time drinking beer, chatting about the financials, thinking about the business model, and deciding how we could better market the company.

One day Mike called me and said, "Brian? Are you sitting down?"

"No, what's up?"

He said, "I think you should sit down."

"I'll stand, but can you tell me what's going on?"

Mike said, "I'm going into competition against you."

"That's not funny, Mike. You're kidding, right?"

"No. I'm serious."

"When?"

"We're hitting the road tomorrow with our first truck."

Mike's betrayal of our friendship hurt, but what happened next hurt even worse.

It soon became painfully obvious to me that "The Rubbish Boys" and "738-JUNK" felt like two different brands to most people. When I would meet someone at a party and they asked, "What do you do for a living?" and I answered, "I've got a junk-removal business," they would often say, "Oh, are you the guy behind Trashbusters?"

Ouch.

I had been in the business for six years and Mike's company was already better known than mine. So I began to think in reactionary ways (which is always a mistake). "How do we take down their signs? How do we get in their way? How do we hit them where it hurts?"

But Mike and his Trashbusters were just proactively trying to grow their business. I was focused on them, and they were focused on them. No one was focused on me.

Finally, I calmed down and started to think about my own company instead of theirs. And then I consolidated my name and phone number into 1-800-GOT-JUNK?.

And soon, Trashbusters changed their phone number to 1-800-RID-OF-IT.

They unknowingly made the same mistake I had made, and it turned out to be their fatal flaw. Trashbusters/1-800-RID-OF-IT was now a company with a split personality. They had diluted their brand.

It wasn't long before we were huge and they were gone.

> The important lesson here is that when I began to think about my own business instead of being distracted by theirs, I began to think more valuable thoughts. I began recruiting better people. I began sharing my vision of the future with everyone on my team. I got better at marketing. I got better at customer service. We began growing into different cities.

That's when my mind began to move into an attitude of gratitude. I became grateful that Mike had awakened me from my slumber.

I would not have expanded into the US as quickly or gotten the trademarks for 1-800-GOT-JUNK? if Mike hadn't awakened me.

Thanks, Mike. Because of you, we upped our game, strengthened our culture, and became a unified team of people championing a vision and a cause. We found our company story and our purpose. We were in the business of making people happy!

8

THE MOMENT THE UNIVERSE CONSPIRED TO ASSIST ME

IT WAS SEPTEMBER 17, 1998, AND I WAS DEPRESSED. 1-800-GOT-JUNK? was eight years old and the company had hit a ceiling after growing to $1 million in revenue. I couldn't get beyond that number. Nothing I did seemed to make a difference.

I was in a doom loop.

"I don't have a college degree."

"I don't have enough operating capital."

"I'm not sure I'm the kind of person who can build a company."

The future was murky and unclear.

But when I created my Painted Picture, the future became clear, bright, and dazzling!

The Painted Picture is a simple visualization technique I created that September while sitting on a dock outside my parents' summer cottage.

Instead of worrying about what wasn't possible, I painted a picture in my head of what I was trying to make happen. I closed my eyes and envisioned how I wanted 1-800-GOT-JUNK? to look, feel, and act by New Year's Eve 2003.

I leaped ahead in my mind to a day five years later.

For the first time ever, I went into extreme detail. When the picture was complete in my mind, I turned it into a one-page document, blew it up, and framed it in our headquarters for everyone to see.

I listed not only tangible business achievements like the number of franchises we would have and the quality of our trucks, but also more sensory details, like how our team would describe our company to their family members, and what our customers would say they loved most about working with us.

In the five years that followed, roughly 96 percent of what I wrote that day had come to pass, including my dream of appearing on Oprah!

I've shared this simple technique with thousands of others, many who have gone on to build large companies. And I still use it religiously.

> Vision + goal setting + accountability + storytelling = a Painted Picture.

WHAT SCIENCE SAYS ABOUT VISUALIZATION

1. Visualize first. Then plan.

People typically think about goal setting in one of two ways:

1. Pie-in-the-sky hopes and dreams

2. Nuts-and-bolts strategic planning

According to more than two hundred scientific studies, the best way to achieve real results is to utilize both types of visualization. This is known as mental contrasting. By following up your pie-in-the-sky Painted Picture with nuts-and-bolts strategic planning, you'll have both the inspiration and the game plan you need to reach your desired destination.

Note: It's highly important that you do your pie-in-the-sky visualization and your nuts-and-bolts strategic planning in different places. To create your Painted Picture, you need to be inspired and unconstrained so you can connect with what really drives you.

Leave the x's and o's of your business plan for a later day when you begin the process of strategic planning.

2. Company growth begins with a clear vision.

Vision is a core component of every successful leader. A clear vision will impact the performance of your people and the outcome of your organization.

In a study of 183 entrepreneurs (with an average revenue of $2.5 million), the average growth of companies with a vision was more than double the growth of companies without a vision.

3. When you tell yourself a story about the future, it changes the way you think.

Once your mind has seen the future, your subconscious works 24/7 to make that future come to pass. The universe conspires to assist you. Human beings are narrative creatures. Great stories are not only easy for us to remember, but they also alter our beliefs. When we get caught up in a story, our doubts disappear. Our brains are wired to pay attention to stories and remember them.

Your Painted Picture is a vividly detailed story about the future you are going to create. After it has electrified you, it will electrify your team.

4. The details of your Painted Picture make it easier for you—and everyone else—to prioritize it and make sacrifices for it.

Most of us have trouble sacrificing something in the present in return for something larger in the future.

In the famous Stanford marshmallow experiment, children were given a marshmallow and told that if they could wait fifteen minutes to eat it, they would receive a second marshmallow. About 70 percent ate the first marshmallow right away. When Stanford followed up thirty years later, they noticed that the kids who waited the fifteen minutes for the second marshmallow had scored an average of 210 points higher on the SAT and had gone on to have much more productive and successful careers.

Availability bias is the cognitive bias that focuses on the pleasure of eating the marshmallow immediately. Our brain can imagine that pleasure far more readily than the relatively weak pleasure of a promised future reward.

Successful people are the ones who have figured out how to distract themselves from the concrete short-term pleasure of eating the marshmallow and focus instead on an abstract, longer-term larger reward.

The Painted Picture brings the future into focus, making it easier for people to sample those future pleasures in their mind.

5. Sharing a vision publicly creates internal pressure to make it a reality.

The real power of a Painted Picture is unleashed whenever you share it. Public commitment, as documented by researcher Robert Cialdini, is an incredibly effective technique to get people to follow through with what they say. In one study where potential voters in an election were asked to publicly share if they were going to vote and why, voter turnout increased by 25 percent the following day.

When you say it publicly, your brain says, "Well, I guess we're really going to do this!"

> If you are confident enough to state what you really want out of your business, and you're devoted enough to pursue those goals through thick and thin, there's no telling what you can achieve.

6. Revisit your Painted Picture daily.

The more often you visit your Painted Picture, the easier it becomes to accomplish it. This phenomenon is called the mere exposure effect: the more we look at something new, the more we develop a preference for it and have good feelings about it.

9

HOW TO CREATE YOUR OWN PAINTED PICTURE

MAKING YOUR OWN PAINTED PICTURE IS SIMPLE:

1. Retreat

2. Visualize

3. Ask

Retreat: Find a quiet space where you don't have any distractions. Bring a notebook.

Visualize: Move yourself five years into the future. If you have a five-year-old child, imagine your child is now ten. Imagine yourself five years older as well. Once you've transported yourself to that place, look at your happy life and your successful business. Write down the details of what you see.

Ask: Once you've transported yourself to that place, ask your future self some questions that will help you "crystal ball" the future.

1. What things did I do five years ago that really paid off?

2. Why were they the right things to do?

3. What was it that almost kept me from doing those things?

When you return from your trip five years from now, you will know exactly what your future looks like. Then you can start building the team and strategy that will help get you there.

10

CUSTOMER EXPERIENCE

Sperry Rand invented computers, but computers never made them any money.

Bill Gates did not invent computers. He made them easier for customers to use.

Steve Jobs did not invent computers. He made them even easier for customers to use.

Ray Kroc did not invent fast food. He just saw what the McDonald brothers were doing in their only, little, owner-operated location, and thought if he could buy the business, he could duplicate it and make it easy for customers to buy breakfast, lunch, and dinner.

The biggest of the big agree on this one thing: make it easy for the customer to do business with you.

When Jeff Bezos secured the patent for "1-Click" ordering in 1999, it made Amazon.com the champion of hassle-free online shopping. Their exclusive control of 1-Click ordering gave them an extraordinary advantage until September 12, 2017, when that patent finally expired.

The idea that customers could enter their billing, shipping, and payment information just once and forever thereafter just click a button? Wow! That epitomized "make it easy for the customer to do business with you."

When I asked customers what 1-800-GOT-JUNK? could do to make their experience easier, they said, "I want someone who will show up, and show up on time."

People were worried that we would be like the proverbial cable company. "You've got to be home on this particular day. No, we can't narrow it down any closer than that. You've got to be home all day."

As the team at 1-800-GOT-JUNK? worked harder to be there precisely when we promised, customers rewarded us with their loyalty and began recommending us to their friends.

People often say, "The customer is always right," but that never rang true to me. I believe that if you take good care of your people, your people will take good care of your customers. And happy customers grow your reputation, your brand, and your profits.

The promise of the 1-800-GOT-JUNK? brand is clean, shiny trucks, friendly, uniformed drivers, and speedy, stress-free service.

I said, "We're going to be a globally admired brand."

"Brian, that's crazy. Why not start with being a Vancouver-admired brand?"

"No, it's got to be so big that it needs all of us working together to accomplish the impossible."

"Who do you mean when you say, 'All of us?'"

"I mean all of us and all of the 1-800-GOT-JUNK? franchise partners in all of the cities around the world. We are bigger and better together."

"We have franchise partners in other cities?"

"We will."

Today, when you look at 1-800-GOT-JUNK? in Canada, the United States, and Australia, we are definitely admired in those countries. And we're beginning to get emails from Europe from people who admire our company culture.

Waiting all day for the cable guy is hard. And not being able to reach someone in the truck when you've got a question is hard. We decided to take away that friction by making it easy for customers to book online in less than sixty seconds and have our team show up within ninety minutes.

We take away their junk, sweep up, and leave a clean, happy, open space.

It's a little bit like Amazon's 1-Click experience.

> **Whatever business you choose to be in, you are going to have to figure out how to provide value to your customer by solving problems—never creating them.**

Revolutionize the customer's experience in your category.

Take very little of their time.

Make it easy.

"We make junk disappear. All you have to do is point."

Can you think of a better way to say, "Full-service junk removal"?

This idea of junk magically "disappearing" when you point your finger at it is a good example of "Magical Thinking." This may seem counterintuitive, but in the words of legendary ad man Rory Sutherland, "All powerful messages must contain an element of absurdity, illogicality, costliness, disproportion, inefficiency, scarcity, difficulty, or extravagance."

In other words, a message isn't a message, and a story isn't a story, unless it contains something new, surprising, and different.

Keep that in mind if you don't want your ads to be boring.

11

QUIT ADDING. IT'S TIME TO MULTIPLY.

You're staring at a massive, metal disk, mounted horizontally on a vertical axle. It takes determination and dedication to get it to move. And it takes patience to gain momentum.

That flywheel is your business. Your job is to get it spinning as fast as possible because momentum—mass times velocity—is what causes it to throw profits at you.

In the early days of any startup, your flywheel is at a standstill. It will take tremendous effort to get it to budge. You push with everything you've got until the flywheel begins to inch forward. You're almost exhausted when your flywheel completes its first 360-degree turn.

The second turn is a little bit easier. It takes a lot of work, but at last you complete your second rotation.

You keep pushing. Three turns, four turns, five, six.

You're no longer counting. Now you're pushing as you run. And finally, you've broken through!

Vision-People-Systems, Culture-Story-Experience. This is the push-push-push, push-push-push that causes your business to fly.

Each push on your spinning flywheel benefits from the momentum of the previous five pushes.

There are six pushes in all: *Vision-People-Systems, Culture-Story-Experience.*

The idea is that if you push any of these six touchpoints, the entire flywheel benefits from it.

It requires a lot of effort to get a flywheel moving, but once it is spinning and has some momentum, it gets easier and easier to make it spin faster and faster.

Vision-People-Systems, Culture-Story-Experience.

It's like the snowball effect. A snowball rolling down a hill gets progressively bigger until it becomes impossible to stop. The difference is that a flywheel never reaches the bottom of the hill. It can go faster and faster forever. *Vision-People-Systems, Culture-Story-Experience.*

The magic of a business flywheel is that these incremental pushes don't just add up:

$1 + 2 + 3 + 4 + 5 + 6 = \textbf{21}$

Instead, they multiply and go exponential:

$1 \times 2 \times 3 \times 4 \times 5 \times 6 = \textbf{720}$

$\times 1 \times 2 \times 3 \times 4 \times 5 \times 6 = \textbf{518,400}$

$\times 1 \times 2 \times 3 \times 4 \times 5 \times 6 = \textbf{373,248,000}$

$\times 1 \times 2 \times 3 \times 4 \times 5 \times 6 = \textbf{268,738,560,000}$

And now you understand Amazon.

> *"If there's one reason we have done better than our peers in the Internet space over the last six years, it is because we have been focused like a laser on customer experience, and that really does matter, I think, in any business."*
>
> **—Jeff Bezos,** Founder of Amazon

12

YOU WANT TO START WITH A BLANK SHEET OF PAPER? OKAY!

THESE ARE THE THREE THINGS TO REMEMBER IF YOU ARE attempting to do what has never been done.

1. DETERMINATION

People hear the story of how 1-800-GOT-JUNK? was featured on *Oprah* back when she ruled the world, and they think, "Well, you made a phone call and you got lucky."

The true story is that Tyler Wright made call after call, month after month, to Oprah's booking agent. And then one day when Tyler called, they said, "Oh, we just read about 1-800-GOT-JUNK? yesterday in *USA Today*."

Our competitor, Trashbusters, was in that same *USA Today* article, but they didn't have anyone with the determination of Tyler Wright burning up the phone lines each day.

That *USA Today* story happened because someone there read about us in *Fortune* magazine.

The *Fortune* story happened because reporter Adam Lashinsky saw a 1-800-GOT-JUNK? truck in San Mateo County while he was on his way to a party, and when he got there, they were talking about 1-800-GOT-JUNK?. He did a little research and said, "I think I should write about these guys."

Remember what I told you earlier about human capital and how it will buy you things that money cannot? Tyler Wright was extraordinary human capital. You might remember him from my first book, *WTF?! (Willing to Fail)*. His enthusiasm and determination made him a public relations superstar. It wasn't education. It wasn't training. His superpowers were his audacity, his belief in our company, and his determination.

Tyler convinced several of the biggest journalists in America to write stories about our fledgling little company and to interview me on television. Tyler Wright believed that nothing was impossible.

When he finally got around to scheduling a vacation for himself, Tyler went on a hike alone in the wilderness and was never seen again. A massive search was undertaken to find him, with people combing the brush and helicopters filling the sky, but the only thing they ever found was a single footprint from one of his size sixteen shoes.

Tyler was my friend and an important contributor to our success.

I miss him every day.

2. EXPERIMENTATION

My secret belief (well, secret up until now) is that your willingness to experiment, your vision, and your insatiable curiosity, is what attracts human capital to you.

One day I received one of those old-fashioned View-Masters in the mail. It had one of those little cardboard circles in it with those dual transparencies that look amazing when you hold the View-Master up to your eyes.

I held it up to my eyes and saw nothing but random-colored dots, so I pressed the lever on the side, *ker-chunk, ker-chunk, ker-chunk,* and just got more colored dots. So I handed it to my COO at the time, Cameron Herold, and said, "What's up with this? Some guy from New York sent it with a note asking if he could fly to Vancouver to meet us."

Cameron looked into the View-Master and said, "Some of the colored dots spell out 'Vision.'" And then he looked at the name of the person who sent it, and said, "But this Simon Sinek fellow had no way of knowing that you're color-blind."

I told Simon that we would be delighted to meet him, so he flew from New York to Vancouver and slept on my couch.

Keep in mind that this was long before he was famous, and I'm pretty sure Simon Sinek isn't sleeping on couches anymore.

Of all the things that Simon and I did together, the thing that inspired me the most was when he read out loud to me something Steve Jobs had written.

Here it is, laid out and punctuated exactly like the original that Steve Jobs laid out and punctuated on an old typewriter.

Here's to the crazy ones,

the misfits,

the rebels,

the troublemakers,

the round pegs in the square holes…

the ones who see things differently—

they're not fond of rules… and they have no
respect for the status quo.

You can quote them,

disagree with them,

glorify or vilify them,

about the only thing you can't do

is ignore them

because they change things…

they push the human race forward,

and while some may see them

as the crazy ones,

we see genius,

because the people who are crazy enough

to think

they can change the world,

are the ones who do.

To say this inspired me is an understatement; it rocked my world. It got me all lit up about what was possible for my business if we continued to innovate, stay curious, and experiment. Steve's words still remind me to continue pushing and to never stop searching for a like-minded, crazy crew to do it with.

3. INNOVATION

"What if every cell phone had a camera in it? No! Let's make it a video camera! A video camera! And we'll also..."

If you Google the word "innovation" and read all the conflicting definitions, you'll soon be as confused as a termite in a yo-yo.

Chuck Frey, author of *The Mind Mapping Manifesto*, came together with Hitendra Patel, a celebrated coach of emerging leaders in new and fast-growth businesses, to offer this analysis of innovation:

> At first glance, the responses from our experts about the definition of innovation appear different and divergent. A closer review shows that they are in violent agreement but just stated in different ways. It makes sense why the definition of innovation is still misunderstood.

All the experts pointed out that innovation must (a) deliver some positive outcome whether it is tangible value, creation of a new market or a competitive advantage and (b) that the actions required to deliver this value must be new to the company.

Some experts mentioned that innovation applied to stakeholders across the value chain, while a few focused on end customers and markets. What is clear to us is that these narrower boundaries are more defined by the work experience of our experts. Since all our experts are working in the innovation space, we combined the responses to say that innovation does apply across the value chain.

Perhaps the simplest definition of innovation is creating new value and/or capturing value in new ways.

I think maybe world-renowned speaker and innovation facilitator Dr. Ken Hudson offers the definition that resonates with me the most:

Innovation is the creation, development and implementation of a new product, process or service, with the aim of improving efficiency, effectiveness or competitive advantage.

Do you remember what I was saying about the six pushes on the flywheel of business?

Vision-People-Systems, Culture-Story-Experience.

Vision-People-Systems, Culture-Story-Experience.

Vision-People-Systems, Culture-Story-Experience.

> Innovation is a product of Experimentation.
>
> Experimentation is a product of Vision.
>
> Your People perform the Experiments within your Systems.
>
> These Experiments and Innovations become part of Culture.
>
> Your Story is enriched by these Experiments, and
>
> Your customer's Experience is made better through each Innovation.

But don't worry about keeping track of the exact sequence of how it works. Just trust that it does work and never quit pushing that flywheel.

Vision-People-Systems, Culture-Story-Experience.

Vision-People-Systems, Culture-Story-Experience.

Vision-People-Systems, Culture-Story-Experience.

WARNING:

Nicola Tesla, Preston Tucker, and Vincent Van Gogh were geniuses of **determination** who **experimented** and created fantastic **innovations** in their chosen professions. But none of them ever received their reward.

The odds are against you when you start with nothing but a dream.

But if you are convinced that it's impossible for you to be happy unless you start with a blank sheet of paper, welcome to the club! You are, without a doubt, one of the Crazy Ones.

13

HOW TO CHOOSE A BUSINESS TO START FROM SCRATCH

WHEN RAY BARD RETIRED, HE HAD THE MOST SUCCESSFUL track record of any publisher of nonfiction books in the world. More than 50 percent of all the books he published became *New York Times* and *Wall Street Journal* bestsellers.

Ray's got a graph explaining the kinds of books that sell in large volumes and which ones don't. And when I saw it I thought it applies to being in business, too.

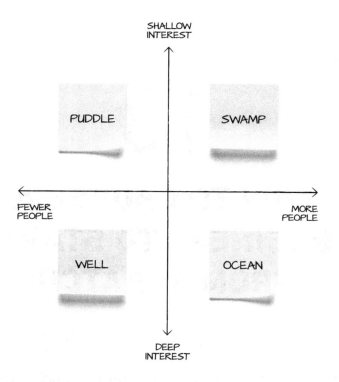

The horizontal line represents how many people are interested.

Extreme left is a small number of people. Extreme right is a vast number of people.

The vertical line represents the depth of their interest.

Upwards is shallower interest. Downwards is deeper interest.

These intersecting lines create an intersection graph with four quadrants.

The upper left quadrant is a Puddle: few people, shallow interest.

The upper right quadrant is a Swamp: lots of people, shallow interest.

The lower left quadrant is a Well: narrow interest, but deep.

The lower right quadrant is an Ocean: lots of people, deep interest.

Ray said, "You obviously can't make money with a book that was written for a Puddle audience. And it's easy to be fooled by a Swamp because it looks huge and a lot of people are interested. *But their interest isn't deep enough to read a book about it.* Market to a Swamp and you'll go broke, but you can make a lot of money by shouting in a Well."

And then he told a story about it. "Years ago, I met a woman who wrote a book about the care and feeding of Quarter Horses. She priced it at $69.95. That's a lot of money for a book today, but it was an enormous amount of money back then, and the category was very narrow. But Quarter Horses aren't cheap to purchase or to own. There is the cost of pasture and stable and veterinary bills and saddles and equipment, and that horse will consume a lot of your time, if you own one. So the interest is very deep. The American Quarter Horse Association has nearly a quarter million members. And a hundred thousand copies at seventy dollars a book is seven million dollars."

His point? There is a lot of money to be made in a Well, but you don't want to fall into the trap of being cost-competitive. You've got to make a lot of profit per customer when you appeal to a narrow group of people.

But then he said, "If you can write a book to an Ocean category, you can sell a lot of books. A whole lot of books."

Like I said, Ray was talking about books, but his graph is also true for business opportunities.

If you were going to sell new cars, would you rather sell Ferraris or Fords?

Ferrari sells 8,400 new cars per year, worldwide. At the time of this writing, a new Portofino is $215,000 at the low end of the product line, and a new SF90 Stradale is $615,000 at the high end. If we assume an average price of $400,000, then Ferrari sells about $3.5 billion in new cars every year.

Compare that to the $160 billion in Fords that are sold each year. And that doesn't include cars built by Chevy, Dodge, Toyota, Nissan, Kia, or Honda.

"If you sell to the classes, you'll live with the masses.

"But if you sell to the masses, you'll live with the classes."

《 When you want to start a business from a blank sheet of paper, sell to an Ocean category, if you can.

Or at least sell to a deeply interested Well.

Be careful not to be fooled by a Swamp. 》

14

AMAZING THINGS HAPPEN WHEN YOU FIND YOUR YODA

IN ANY HERO'S JOURNEY, THERE'S A GURU, OLD MAN IN the woods, or good witch to prepare you for the next leg of your adventure. Luke Skywalker met Obi-Wan Kenobi, and then he encountered Yoda, who gave him the wisdom he needed to complete his journey.

A smart person makes a mistake, learns from it, and never makes that mistake again. But a wise person looks for a smart person and learns how to avoid that mistake altogether.

When I joined YPO (Young Presidents' Organization) many years ago, I encountered three types of people, who each got their start in business a different way.

1. Entrepreneurs: Someone who finds an opportunity no one's thought of and takes the risk of starting a business from scratch. Think Brian Chesky, inventor of the billion-dollar home-sharing platform Airbnb; the founders of Casper Sleep, Philip Krim, Neil Parikh, T. Luke Sherwin, Jeff Chapin, and Gabriel Flateman; and Sara Blakely, who revolutionized undergarments with Spanx.

2. Hired guns: A professional with extensive outside experience, hired to fill in a flat spot. It's Sheryl Sandberg to Facebook's Mark Zuckerberg or Tim Cook to Apple's Steve Jobs.

3. Old money: Someone whose family has a long legacy in business, like the Waltons. You might know them as the Walmart family.

Although these presidents ran their businesses differently, there was one thing they all agreed on.

Whenever I would ask, "What stage of business growth is the hardest? Is it $1 million? Is it $10 million? $100 million? A billion?" Without exception, every billion-dollar president said, "The hardest is $1 million. The easiest is a billion."

When I asked them why a billion is easier, they answered, "Because you have momentum on your side. Your flywheel is spinning and you have a team of people helping you so you don't have to split your attention among a hundred different things like you did back when you were doing your first million. And now you've got systems and processes, so every little thing is dialed in for maximum efficiency. You're no longer working *in* your business; you're working *on* your business."

The presidents I encountered at YPO were my first real guides in the world of entrepreneurship.

15

KNOW WHEN IT'S TIME FOR PLAN B

❝When you look at Fortune 500 companies, it's easy to assume that each of those companies had a fabulous plan and they executed it perfectly.

But in truth, the majority of those companies abandoned Plan A and succeeded only after they switched to Plan B, C, or D.❞

This is a fundamental reality of almost every startup: "Plan A was a great idea, but it didn't work quite the way we thought it would."

The companies who succeed are the ones who have the financial and emotional staying power to admit they were wrong and start all over.

Martin Luther King Jr. didn't plan to give the "I Have a Dream" speech the day those 250,000 people gathered for the March on Washington. Bob Dylan, Joan Baez, and Peter, Paul, and Mary all sang to the crowd. As an afterthought, gospel singer Mahalia Jackson was added to the list. She was standing close to her friend, Martin Luther King Jr., because she was scheduled to sing right after his speech.

MLK had prepared a speech about how America had written a bad check, and that check had bounced. But soon after he began to speak, he knew it wasn't going well. He knew he wasn't connecting, but he didn't know what to do. That's when his friend Mahalia Jackson said, "Tell them about the dream, Martin. Tell them about the dream."

MLK and Mahalia locked eyes for a moment. Watch the video. Mahalia had heard Martin describe his painted picture of a future America and it electrified her.

"Tell them about the dream, Martin. Tell them about the dream."

Plan B is launched when MLK shuffles his papers together and slides them off to the side.

MLK deserves our applause for crafting and delivering that mighty speech, but Mahalia Jackson was the sage who gave him wise counsel in his moment of need.

Fred DeLuca named his first sandwich shop "Pete's Submarines" to acknowledge the $1,000 startup loan from his friend Peter Buck. The store was not a success. DeLuca realized he had to change the name of his store when listeners thought he was saying "Pizza Marines" in his local radio ads.

Plan B turned out differently. When Fred passed away in 2015, his Plan B had spawned 44,268 independently owned Subway franchises in 110 countries. He and his $1,000 investor, Peter Buck, were each worth $3.5 billion according to his obituary in the *New York Times*.

Not a bad return on a $1,000 investment!

Paul Guy had been incredibly successful at College Pro Painters, so I recruited him to help me build a franchise program. He understood student franchising, so we took all of Vancouver, fifteen territories, and found a college student in each territory and began preparing them to run a summer business.

We would work from January to March recruiting students from universities, spend April getting them ready, and in May, June, July, and August, they'd run the business. Then in September, we'd begin shutting them down. It was a ton of work and we made no money. But all fifteen of our student franchise partners said, "I made so much money! I want to do it again next year!"

Our mistake was creating a business model that coincided when students were on summer break, when we should have focused on the customer, who wants full-service junk removal year-round.

It was time for Plan B. It was time to create a grown-up franchise—a twelve-month operation.

Toronto is to Vancouver what New York is to Los Angeles. So when Paul Guy volunteered to become franchise partner number one in Toronto, on the other side of the continent, he had none of the benefits of our local Vancouver fame. But because he learned from my experience in Vancouver, where it took me eight years to reach $1 million, Paul did it in his very first year in Toronto.

"Hey! We're coast-to-coast!"

"Really? How many locations do you have?"

"Including that one?"

"Yeah."

"Two."

Today Paul Guy owns 1-800-GOT-JUNK? franchises in Toronto, Saskatchewan, Winnipeg, New York City, Charlotte, Chicago, New Jersey, Raleigh, Las Vegas, Nashville, Vermont, Brisbane, Melbourne, and Sydney with combined revenues of more than $76 million per year.

Plan B worked out a lot better than Plan A.

16

ANOTHER EXAMPLE OF KNOWING WHEN IT IS TIME FOR PLAN B

Sean Jones agreed to meet me for breakfast at a little three-dollar diner. We never had to worry about being interrupted, because it's the last place on earth anyone would ever expect to find either one of us.

1-800-GOT-JUNK? was doing about $100 million a year, but I felt we'd hit another ceiling on growth. I enjoyed talking to Sean because he had purchased Spence Diamonds from Doug Spence and then refined the operations of those seven engagement ring stores until he had them functioning like a finely tuned, well-oiled machine.

Sean's operational excellence and intense focus on customer service took Spence Diamonds to the next level, and then the next. And his perfectly executed in-house manufacturing process allowed him to create high-quality inventory on demand, resulting in a 27x inventory turn in a category where most stores can't get beyond a 2x turn. Basically, he sold a LOT more diamonds in the same amount of time, in the same amount of retail space.

But then Sean hit a ceiling. He could see more customers out there, but he couldn't figure out how to get them to walk through his doors. He hired ad agency after ad agency and did exactly what each one of them told him to do, but his sales remained flat, flat, flat.

Sean Jones was an old man in the woods for me.

Sean told me how he finally broke through that ceiling. He said, "I flew 1,871 miles and spent several thousand dollars to speak to a completely insane marketing guy. Everything I had ever heard about him frightened me, but he had an incredible record of success. It took me three months to get his gatekeeper to even accept my money and give me a date to meet him."

"You're kidding."

"No, I'm serious. I flew down there on the appointed day and after listening to me for a few hours, he said, 'I can grow your same-store business by 28 percent in the first twelve months, and we'll grow a lot more than that in year number two, and then in year three, we'll find out if you're tall enough to ride this roller coaster. But you're going to have to let me make three changes in your marketing that you're not going to want to make.'"

"What did he tell you to change?" I asked. "Your ad budget or the pricing of your engagement rings?"

"Neither," Sean answered. "He left the ad budget alone. In fact, he didn't even change how or where we spent our ad dollars. And he made no suggestions about our profit margin. He changed only what we were saying in our ads."

"And it gave you a 28 percent lift in year one?!"

"Yes, from ad copy alone! And in year two, we began to really skyrocket," Sean said. "You've gotta talk to him."

But I quickly learned that Sean's crazy ad guy didn't necessarily want to talk to *me*. His gatekeeper told me that it cost $7,500 in advance, a flight to Austin, and a drive to a secluded castle (yes, castle!) to meet the Wizard of Ads. Even then, she informed me it was highly unlikely he'd write any ads for us—he'd probably recommend us to one of his partners instead.

But I had a gut feeling that this could change the business and catapult it to the next level. And frankly, my curiosity was piqued; who was this guy?

So I paid the money, flew 1,871 miles, drove to the castle, and discovered that the gatekeeper was right: he didn't want to work with us. It was only after I shared our "whatever it takes" approach to PR that landed us on *Good Morning America,* the *New York Times,* and A&E's *Hoarders,* that the Wiz changed his mind. He liked the buzz we were generating and saw the passion we had for sharing our story.

I flew home knowing exactly what I needed to do to get beyond my own ceiling. And after that meeting, our business doubled in just under four years.

> ❝ Sometimes, the perfect Plan B will come along in an unexpected way. It might even come from a crazy person who rejects traditional wisdom. Crazy people say, "Traditional wisdom is often more tradition than wisdom. ❞

And I agree with them...which probably makes me crazy, too!

17

WHAT TO DO WHEN PLAN B DOESN'T WORK

WHEN I WAS READY TO FRANCHISE 1-800-GOT-JUNK?, I reached out to a dozen franchise experts who said, "This can't be franchised."

Their response reminded me of all those times I called the press and was told, "This isn't a story that we would be interested in."

When an expert tells you no, don't think of it as a door slamming in your face. That expert has given you a gift— if you can unwrap it.

When the press said no about doing a story on my company, I would say, "I can accept that. But I would consider it a huge favor if you would tell me what's missing. What needs to be different for this to be a story?"

But note: when you ask that question, you've got to make it clear that you are not setting them up for a debate. They need to trust that you are seeking to understand, rather than to be understood.

Sometimes those people will answer your question. And then you will know something extremely important that you didn't know before.

When *USA Today* said, "No, we're not interested in your story," I embraced what they taught me, learned from it, and in my next call, they said yes! That call was to the *New York Times*.

The press taught me how to pitch a story to the press.

When the first eleven franchising experts told me no, I said, "I can accept that. But it would be a huge favor if you would be willing to tell me what's missing. What would need to be different for this business to be viable as a franchise?"

Those franchising experts, one by one, taught me how to create a successful franchise.

"Every time you are told, "No," ask yourself, "Why did they choose to say no? What's missing?" But remember: they won't give you an answer unless they are confident you are only trying to understand what you need to correct. They need to know that you are not trying to get them to change their mind."

18

FAILURE IS NOT A PERMANENT CONDITION

ANY BASKETBALL PLAYER WHO SHOOTS AND MISSES HAS failed. But are they a failure?

Any football team that punts the ball has failed to make the requisite ten yards. But are they a failure?

The baseball player who bats .400 is the league batting champion, even though they failed to get on base six out of every ten times they went to the plate.

If you don't fail occasionally, you're not taking enough chances. But if you fail too often, you won't survive the learning curve.

1. Successful companies differentiate themselves in ways that customers actually care about.

2. It helps if the name of the company reflects the wonderful thing they do.

I hit the bullseye on both of these with WOW 1 DAY PAINTING.

A customer wants the rooms of their house painted. That's no secret. Every painting company knows this. What they fail to realize is that those customers are not looking forward to the ongoing disruption to their household. This is what causes them to be reluctant about saying, "Yes. Now is the time."

In my Painted Picture for WOW 1 DAY PAINTING, I imagined a painting company with such highly refined systems, processes, job planning, and techniques that a team could paint your entire house in one day. You would leave for work in the morning, and when you return, every room of your home has been painted perfectly, in each of the colors you wanted, and all the furniture is back in place.

And it all happened in a single day. WOW.

We created that brand, but for some reason, the business wasn't taking off, even a few years in.

Finally, a friend said, "Your brand colors—navy blue and orange—remind me of a college football team." Then another friend said, "Brian, a painting brand needs to build trust with homeowners. How would you feel if a group of guys walked into your home dressed in penitentiary orange?"

It never occurred to me that our painters were pulling up and unloading a team that looked like they were part of a prison work-release program.

I suddenly realized that people were not buying franchises as quickly as I thought they would because customers weren't connecting with the business. We were building a premium brand and offering a premium service, but the image we were projecting didn't stack up.

Fast-forward to a much-needed family vacation in Florence, Italy. I was ordering gelato when I looked down and saw a rectangular tub full of lime gelato with lime slices arranged in a smiley face. The gelato was smiling at me and it was impossible not to smile back.

I took a photo of it and sent it to FreeBird Agency, who does all of our branding. Noel and David created the lime-green-and-white logo and happy uniforms that rocketed WOW 1 DAY PAINTING into the stratosphere.

We spent hundreds of thousands of dollars to rebrand WOW 1 DAY PAINTING with an all-new look and feel. The franchise partners all agreed it was the best money they ever spent, because that franchise took off like a jet from an aircraft carrier.

> « Your business model has to speak to a felt need, but your marketing has to connect to the heart. »

Part of your marketing is your name.

Part of your marketing is your logo and your brand colors.

Part of your marketing is the personality radiated by the words you use.

You might not get it right the first time, but you've got to get it right before you can lift off the runway. Your skycraft needs wind beneath its wings and the name of that wind is marketing.

19

LOOK AT YOUR BUSINESS FROM THE CUSTOMER'S PERSPECTIVE

When Steve Jobs returned to Apple in 1997 to save that company from the brink of bankruptcy, he said,

> One of the things I've always found is that you've got to start with the customer experience and work backwards to the technology. You can't start with the technology and try to figure out where you're going to try to sell it. And I've made this mistake probably

more than anybody else in this room. And I've got the scar tissue to prove it. And I know that it's the case. And as we have tried to come up with a strategy—and a vision for Apple, um, it started with "What incredible benefits can we give to the customer? Where can we take the customer?" not, not starting with, "Let's sit down with the engineers and, and figure out what awesome technology we have and then how are we going to market that."

The customer doesn't want fertilizer. They want green grass.

The customer doesn't want a lawn mower. They want a smooth and level lawn.

The customer doesn't want a quarter-inch drill bit. They want quarter-inch holes.

The customer doesn't want junk removal. They want a clean, organized space.

The customer doesn't want a housepainter. They want their walls to be beautiful.

> The customer doesn't want window washing, gutter cleaning, power washing, and Christmas lights. They want a beautiful, sparkling home. 》》

Offer your customer what their heart desires, not what your head tells you they *ought* to want—"if only they understood."

Bad advertising is about you, your company, your product, your service. Good advertising is about the customer, and how your product or service will elevate their happiness and change their world.

This is one of the things the crazy guy told me. There's a lot more, but I'm saving it for another day.

20

TWENTY YEARS IN, I'M STILL LEARNING

You can never be sure whether or not you're making a mistake until later, when the consequences of your decision are in full bloom.

You just have to launch your rocket and keep your fingers crossed.

Launi Skinner had previously been the president of Starbucks. I was incredibly lucky to hire her.

Due to a series of questionable decisions, 1-800-GOT-JUNK? was deeply in debt in 2008. Launi was working on an injection of capital from a private equity group, but it would have cost me more than half my company. I would no longer be in control.

We were just three days away from signing when I said, "This doesn't feel right. I don't know if I can handle letting go of my business."

When the deal was dead and Launi was gone, I had the same feeling that I'd made a terrible mistake, and I'd let my franchise partners down.

Most of them were saying to me, "She was smart. She was unbelievable. How could you let her go?"

A few years later I was nominated for the Ernst and Young Entrepreneur of the Year Award for the third time.

When I showed up to meet the judges to have a private conversation with each of them, I saw that one of them was Launi Skinner. The thought that flashed through my mind was, "I'm doomed. She must hate me!"

After I learned I had won, I ran into one of the other judges. He said, "We were really inspired to hear all the nice things Launi had to say about you and your business."

A friend once said to me,

About 33 percent of the things we worry about never come to pass. Another 33 percent are so inconsequential that they're not really worth our worry. And another 33 percent are things that might come to pass but cannot be changed, no matter how well we worry. This leaves only a tiny percentage that will come to pass, and are important, and can be changed if we take action.

I looked at him and said, "Is that your way of telling me to chill out?"

He just smiled and nodded his head.

There's a lesson buried in that story for you.

I'll let you discover it for yourself.

21

ANOTHER GUIDE, ANOTHER PATH

Greg Brophy started Shred-it, a billion-dollar business. When Launi was gone and I didn't know what to do, I remembered something he told me:

> « Never, ever, ever, ever compromise on the quality of people you bring into your organization. »

Greg knew that my original second-in-command had been one of my best friends, Cameron Herold; I was even the best man at his wedding. Cameron took us from $2 million to $106 million, but we were both "fire, ready, aim" types—and I knew I needed someone to balance out my strengths and weaknesses to take the business even further. It was incredibly tough, but we ended up agreeing to part ways.

When I'd asked Greg why I was having trouble finding the yin to my yang in a COO, he told me, "Brian, you're doing exactly what I did. In fact, you're doing what most entrepreneurs do."

"How so?"

"Most people choose a close friend to be their first chief operating officer. The second time, they go to the other extreme and hire someone based on pedigree, even if they're not necessarily a culture fit. But it never works out.

"The third time, they strike a balance between those two extremes and begin looking for a seasoned professional who is a cultural fit, and with whom they have genuine rapport."

I said, "That sounds like *Goldilocks and the Three Bears*. Did you go through that?"

Greg indicated that he had.

So I took a sheet of paper and drew a line down the middle. On one side I listed all the things I'm good at—things I would not want to let go of and shouldn't. On the other side I listed all the things I'm bad at—things I don't like to do and wish I could let go of (and should).

Then I created a Painted Picture of the COO I was looking for and circulated it among all my most trusted advisors.

In this Painted Picture, I imagined my perfect COO candidate saying,

> I am a high-energy, results-driven leader. People on my team know we play to win. When the goal is clear, I don't let anything get in our way. I work hard to ensure my team is composed of top talent and that their teams each have the right people in the right seats. I develop my people to be their best and to work hard to grow our business—to believe in and realize the possibilities we set. I thrive on having full responsibility for revenue and sales growth.
>
> Sales and marketing have been a core part of any business I have helped build. I am passionate about building strategic plans that translate into results—plans that allow me to lead the charge with focused execution, tight accountability, and frequent celebration.

I am looking to partner with an entrepreneur whose vision is crystal clear, but one who needs an executional COO to help him figure out the HOW to his WHERE. I love Canada and have always wanted to call Vancouver home.

Three people responded to me, who didn't know each other and all lived in very different parts of North America. But *all* of them said, "You're looking for Erik Church."

I met him. I liked him. And he was excited about our future.

Erik proved to be

the right person

at the right time,

doing the right things,

in the right way,

for the right reasons.

Erik quickly helped our team go from $100 million to $500 million. And in five years when we hit one billion, we'll have the party to end all parties!

> Pulling out that sheet of paper and being honest about my strengths and weaknesses was an invaluable exercise. It gave me a chance to focus on what I love and do best, and enabled me to build my team and business.
>
> What's on your sheet of paper?

Greg Brophy is gone now, but I will remember Greg forever.

And my hope for you is that your Yodas will always show up at exactly the right time, just like Sean Jones and Greg Brophy did for me.

22

MAKING MEANING VERSUS MAKING MONEY

ONE OF THE THINGS I LEARNED ON MY JOURNEY IS THAT business is all about people. Your team members are people and your customers are people. You are in the people business.

I said to myself in 1994, "Hold on. I have the wrong people and I haven't been treating them right. If I focus on finding the right people and figure out how to treat them right, what would my business look and feel like then?"

When making money became my secondary goal and I began to focus on making meaning, I began to think and talk about "building something bigger and better together" versus going at it alone. When you understand people's dreams, ambitions, and life goals, it allows you to say, "Here's how the business can help you. Here's how we can help each other."

When you realize that providing a place of work where your people feel like they belong and where they know they're doing great work and learning and growing and developing, then the money floods in like a tsunami. When I shifted away from money as my primary goal, I began making decisions that benefited the bottom line in a much bigger way.

> Happy, highly engaged, grateful people bring in money. Unhappy, disinterested, glass-half-empty people do not.
>
> Guess who has the power to cause your people to become highly engaged and grateful?
>
> You do.

Jack Stack wrote *The Great Game of Business*. Jack is the father of open-book management and profit sharing. He says, "Give people a stake in the outcome." And sometimes he means a financial stake.

After thinking about it, I decided, "After we've hit a base level of profitability that allows us to finance the growth of the company moving forward, we're going to take 20 percent of all profits above that number and allocate that money to our team."

When I involved my entire team in open-book management, they quickly became financially literate. They were more connected to the business when they saw the numbers. They said, "We're spending that many millions of dollars on advertising? Thousands on coffee for our team? I had no idea there were all these expenses involved in running a business!"

They saw the business in a different way when they had a stake in the outcome, and their daily decisions began to shift the business to a sunnier, brighter, more profitable place.

The sooner you realize you're in the people business, the happier you'll be.

Today we pay out more than a million dollars in every profit-sharing session. Our people are being rewarded for their high level of engagement and involvement in the business.

In the summer of 2021, Jeff Bezos, Elon Musk, and Richard Branson each spent billions of dollars to take rides in space that lasted between one and four minutes.

In space, Branson beamed at the video camera and said,

> To all you kids down there, I was once a child with a dream, looking up to the stars. Now I'm an adult in a spaceship with lots of other wonderful adults looking down to our beautiful, beautiful earth.

Within minutes, a meme appeared on Twitter:

> Remember kids: if you study hard, get good grades, go to a good college, get a job, work hard, never take a sick day, live within your means, and do what you're told...then one day your boss might go to space.

In a moment of extreme excitement when he wanted to inspire the next generation, Branson momentarily forgot to talk to his people—his team. And in that one moment, broadcast around the world, some of his people saw it as *his* company and not *their* company. And that hurt.

> When you begin to make meaning instead of just making money—when you empower your people with information and help them see how they can achieve their personal goals by helping the company achieve its goals—your people become more engaged in the business, they stay longer, and the company makes a lot more money.

I'm sure Richard Branson's team forgave him because he's a really great guy at heart.

But I also suspect he would say something different if given a second chance.

23

INSPECT WHAT YOU EXPECT

JACK DALY—THE PROFESSIONAL SALES COACH—IS another guru for me. He's a supersmart guy who has written twenty-one books. One day I called him and said, "Jack, we're having some challenges in our call center. We're just not converting calls into sales like we should."

Jack said, "Well, I don't really do consulting, but I want to come and help you."

A few days later, the phone rang. Jack said, "Okay, I'm in town. So we're starting tomorrow morning, right?"

I said, "Yes, absolutely."

"What time do you want to start?"

I said, "You tell me."

"How's 4:00 a.m.? I'll see you at the Denny's across the street from my hotel."

When I showed up at 4:00 a.m., Jack had already run the ten kilometers around the seawall at Stanley Park and had been waiting for me for fifteen minutes. He said, "We are going to dismiss everyone from their jobs. They're still going to be in the company, but we're going to say, 'You no longer have a position. We're going to figure out your new position later.'"

Then we headed over to the call center where Jack asked, "Brian, who are the most awesome people in the sales center who can coach and train? Which people can be role models for the others?"

I named five people.

Jack called their names and said, "Okay, coaches, one at a time, just like on the playground." Then he pointed at each of them as he said, "You pick first, you second, you third..."

The five coaches each picked their call center agents and then we set up teams and incentives.

That's when Jack told me, "You need to inspect what you expect. Every business trains its people and sets goals. They give their people a plan and then turn them loose. But the mistake most companies make is that they abdicate instead of delegate."

I said, "I need to delegate, not abdicate."

Jack nodded his head yes.

"And I need to inspect what I expect."

He nodded and said, "Give them parameters. Let them know what success is. Then say, 'I'm going to inspect, for your benefit and the benefit of all of us, that you're doing the best job that you can do.'"

On our final day together, Jack and I grabbed some agents in the sales center and said, "You're going to be part of an **Inspect What You Expect** session. We want you to critique the performance of your fellow team members."

We put them in a boardroom where they would listen to a live call that Jack or one of the coaches would make into the call center. Then they'd bring that agent in, give them high fives, and tell them what they did that was great, along with things they could do differently.

Jack Daly catalyzed a culture where you can't just build a new website and leave it. You can't just set and forget your new marketing program, or train your people and never see them again. You have to forever check in. You have to inspect what you expect. And so, to this day, I still call in to each of our brands multiple times a year, and I visit our websites and book online appointments.

People might say, "Well, that's diving in way too deep for a CEO. Don't you trust your team?"

I do trust my team. But our company is big and things can go wrong. When I do these inspections, I occasionally find that our performance is no longer in alignment with my expectations.

If you own an airline, hop on a flight! You need to see firsthand what things are like. And while this seems like common sense, CEOs don't do it often enough.

When I find something broken, people say, "Oh, that's just the Scudamore effect," as though the mistake would not have happened if it had been any other visitor than me.

No, it's just me inspecting what I expect.

To make it more fun, I asked my call center team, "Who runs the best call center?" They decided it was WestJet, the Southwest Airlines of Canada. So we brought several groups of agents into the boardroom and said, "We're going to do a ghost call to 1-800-GOT-JUNK?, and then we're going to do a ghost call to WestJet and vote on who was the friendliest."

And it was always easy to tell.

The day finally came when we did a bunch of calls and the score was five to four, 1-800-GOT-JUNK? over WestJet!

The celebration was epic.

《 Train your people. Inspect what you expect. Compare yourselves with the best. See how you do. If you do it right, it will be an interesting, insightful, fun experience for everyone involved. 》

24

WHAT HAPPENS WHEN YOU FAIL TO INSPECT WHAT YOU EXPECT

BACK IN THE EARLY 2000S, MCDONALD'S REALIZED THEY had lost their focus, so they called on a former guru to help them find it again. He returned to McDonald's with a single objective: "Inspect What You Expect."

In a June 27, 2004, story called "McDonald's Finds Missing Ingredient," *Chicago Tribune* staff reporters David Greising and Jim Kirk wrote:

Fred Turner did not need to look at financial statements to know McDonald's was in trouble. He could taste it.

The man who worked alongside founder Ray Kroc to turn McDonald's Corp. into a global colossus, Turner noticed when penny pinchers at corporate headquarters changed recipes to cut costs. So when McDonald's cheapened the famed "special sauce" on its flagship Big Mac sandwich, Turner knew.

But it wasn't until a new CEO brought him back from retirement 18 months ago to help lead a turnaround at McDonald's that the now 71-year-old Turner learned just how deep the trouble ran.

McDonald's had lost the recipe to the special sauce.

In the annals of marketing, the Big Mac special sauce has a sizzle like Coke's secret formula or Kentucky Fried Chicken's secret blend of 11 herbs and spices. To people inside McDonald's, losing the special sauce meant a loss of connection with the company's very roots.

It didn't take Turner long to find it.

He recalled the name of a California supplier who had helped develop the sauce 36 years ago. The supplier recovered the recipe.

"It's time to make a hamburger the way we used to make a hamburger," Turner said to the 25 restaurant owners on McDonald's Food Improvement Team.

The return of the special sauce was one of hundreds of changes, big and small, that McDonald's made after Fred Turner returned the company to an "Inspect What You Expect" culture. And the result was one of the most stunning turnarounds in corporate history.

25

THE POWER OF
ASKING FOR HELP

I MOVED AROUND A LOT, WENT TO FOURTEEN SCHOOLS, skipped a lot of classes, and got kicked out, so I've always been keenly aware of my lack of formal education.

I was never able to get an MBA—Master's of Business Administration—so I created my own MBA, my Mentor Board of Advisors.

When I read a great book or an article about an entrepreneur, author, or thought leader I felt I could learn from, I put them on my MBA list. You might recognize some of the names, but there are a lot you wouldn't.

Who you put on your list of mentor board of advisors is up to you.

One day I picked up the phone and said, "I just read this book by Michael Gerber. Can I speak to him, please?" My call was rejected time and again, of course, but Michael Gerber finally came to Vancouver to visit our offices. After spending a day with us, he said, "I have never seen anyone 'E-Myth' a business to the degree that you people have!"

I believe authors, public speakers, successful CEOs, and other experts love being asked for help. Put it to the test. Call someone you admire and say, "There is no one in the world as good at what you do. Can I ask you some questions?"

Don't be surprised (and be prepared!) when they say, "Of course you can."

I met most of the people on my mentor board of advisors before any of them had heard of 1-800-GOT-JUNK?, and you can be sure they had never heard of Brian Scudamore.

I had just begun franchising 1-800-GOT-JUNK? when I bumped into a man in the hallway at the International Franchise Association Conference. When I turned to apologize, I saw his name tag. "You're Fred DeLuca? Hi, I'm Brian Scudamore. I love Subway!"

He was busy and had to leave, so I said, "May I, one day, get in touch with you to ask a few questions about how you did what you did?"

Fred gave me his card with his phone number. He talked with me long before my company had grown into anything substantial. Sometimes he would call from his car and leave me a message: "I have to be at a meeting at such and such a time and I've got a one-hour drive to get there. Call me and we'll talk."

And I always did.

Fred didn't call me because I had something to offer him in return. I was just a nobody who was passionate, curious, and deeply appreciative.

But sometimes passion and curiosity are all you need to gain the attention of a giant.

26

WHAT KIND OF ENTREPRENEUR WILL YOU BE?

I'VE HAD OPPORTUNITIES TO MEET SOME OF THE BEST and brightest in business; a few of these titans are listed below. What always strikes me most when I connect with fellow entrepreneurs is how unique they are. Each of them chose a wildly different path to success, but they played to their strengths, trusted their gut, and were always true to themselves.

Who do you resonate with? Why? Maybe there's someone who isn't on the list—add them. Get inspired, understand your *raison d'etre,* and get ready to go forward.

THE "GROW WHERE YOU'RE PLANTED" ENTREPRENEUR

Chip Wilson's mother was a seamstress. With his interests in sports and being outdoors, it was a natural step for him to start sewing apparel for surfers, skaters, and snowboarders. But it was at a yoga class in the '90s when an idea hit: revolutionize athleisure. Using his background in sewing and expertise in functional apparel, he invented a new category with lululemon.

Thanks to Chip's philosophy that, "There's no performance without action. When an opportunity presents itself, take it—no matter where it is," that bright idea turned into a $6 billion empire and turned yoga into an activity for everyone.

《 When your big idea hits, be ready. 》

THE "PASSION PROJECT" ENTREPRENEUR

Tony Hawk started skateboarding when he was nine. He bought his first home and moved out at seventeen—every teenager's fantasy, right? But when skateboarding went out of style in 1991, Tony lost almost everything. At twenty-four years old, he was living on five dollars a day.

But skateboarding was his whole life. So he mortgaged his house to start a skateboard company while he continued to compete. Then he was approached by Sony PlayStation to consult on a struggling Bruce Willis game called *Apocalypse*. When he noticed the movements of the game were true to his real-life skateboarding experience, the blockbuster game *Tony Hawk Pro Skater* was born.

> **You can turn what you love into a business. But be patient.**

THE "EX-CORPORATE" ENTREPRENEUR

Brit Morin is a veteran of Silicon Valley, working at Apple and then at Google under Marissa Mayer. The self-proclaimed nerd had an epiphany in 2011: as adults, women don't have the same creative confidence they had as children. So she left her job and launched Brit + Co, a digital-only platform for women with 130 million monthly followers who have access to how-to courses and DIY creative projects.

Brit was on a trajectory to succeed in the corporate world when she pivoted to do something of her own. Now she's at the helm of a multimillion-dollar empire.

> **You don't have to keep your corporate job if you want to build a legacy of your own.**

THE "CURE YOUR PAIN POINT" ENTREPRENEUR

As legend has it, the idea for Netflix was born out of frustration and a forty-dollar late fee for a Blockbuster VHS tape. Reed Hastings and Marc Randolph decided to revolutionize the movie-rental business with a DVD rental company that would eliminate late fees. In 1997, Netflix was born.

But what happened next is even more incredible. Netflix went on to solve its *own* pain point. "Snail mail" made their DVD delivery windows difficult to predict, and one-day deliveries were nearly impossible to guarantee. When they introduced streaming in 2007, they offered their customers instant satisfaction and revolutionized how we consume content.

> *Sometimes, all you need to get started with a business idea is to identify a common inconvenience. But don't forget to keep looking for pain points and solving them for your customers!*

THE "FRANCHISE KING" ENTREPRENEUR

As you already know, Shaq is a big proponent of the franchise model. At one point or another, he's owned 155 Five Guys restaurants, seventeen Auntie Anne's, and a Krispy Kreme franchise! Maybe it's because the NBA is a franchise, and Shaq got his idea from his time in the game.

Shaq took his ability to learn and try new things and built great teams using formulas proven by others. And now he's the franchise king!

> *You can be an incredible entrepreneur and leader without coming up with something by yourself.*

Chip, Hawk, Brit, Reed, and Shaq all took totally different paths, but they have one thing in common: they got started.

I hope you'll take the leap, too.

27

STARTING FROM A BLANK SHEET OF PAPER, STEP BY STEP

So here we are—already at Chapter 27!

Now it's time to dive into what you need to think about if you're planning to start a business with that blank sheet of paper. Keep in mind, this isn't a step-by-step guide. There are plenty of experts out there who can help you with the nitty-gritty, including Michael Gerber, who wrote *The E-Myth* (a book I highly recommend). But this is an overview of how I approached my own blank sheet of paper.

1. CHOOSE A CATEGORY OF BUSINESS

Will you sell a product, service, or both?

What percentage of the public will ever buy what you sell?

How often will they need to buy it? What is the product purchase cycle?

Will you have to maintain inventory? Who will be your supplier(s)?

2. STUDY YOUR COMPETITION

How well-known are they?

What are they known for?

What are their approximate sales volumes?

How do they advertise?

3. WHAT WILL YOU DO BETTER THAN YOUR COMPETITORS?

How will you be new, surprising, or different? Will you break new ground?

Is this a difference that people will actually care about? Does it speak to a felt need or pain point?

How will you communicate this difference? What captivating phrases will you use?

To which media will you commit the bulk of your ad budget?

What will be the boundaries of your trade area?

4. DETERMINE YOUR PROFIT MARGIN

1. What percentage of each dollar in top-line revenue will be consumed by your costs?

2. If you sell a product, what will be your projected inventory turn? The simplest retail businesses have a 50 percent **gross profit.** This means that 50 percent of each dollar is available to pay all the costs of doing business and make a profit. The other 50 percent is what they paid for the product they sold.

NOTE: If you pay fifty cents for a product and add another fifty cents gross profit, you have added a 100 percent markup. **Markup** is your gross profit expressed as a percentage of your cost of goods. **Gross margin** is your gross profit expressed as a percentage of sales.

A 50 percent markup is a 33 percent gross margin.

A 100 percent markup is a 50 percent gross margin.

A 200 percent markup is a 66.66 percent gross margin.

A 300 percent markup is a 75 percent gross margin.

A 400 percent markup is an 80 percent gross margin.

If you maintain an inventory of $1 million, add a 100 percent markup, and do a 1x annual **inventory turn,** your total sales that year will be $2 million.

If you do a 2x inventory turn (sell all your inventory once, replace it, and sell it again) your annual sales will be $4 million. In that first scenario, you probably went broke. It is hard to survive if you have only a 50 percent gross margin and a 1x inventory turn. In the second scenario, you might survive, but you didn't make much money.

You will occasionally hear of highly successful businesses (Costco, Sam's Club, etc.) that operate on a 15 percent gross profit. Dig a little deeper and you'll find they get at least a 12x inventory turn. In other words, they may invest $1 million in inventory, but they will sell it and make $150,000 gross profit **every month**, and then replace that inventory and make another $150,000 on that same $1 million investment the next month and the next month and the next. At the end of a year, they will have made $1,800,000 in gross profit on an investment of just $1 million *which is still stacked in the warehouse.*

The rule of thumb in a service business is that you must charge at least three times the amount per hour that you are paying your employee. If the employee makes thirty dollars an hour, you must charge at least ninety dollars per hour for their work. If you attempt to charge less than that, you will likely go broke. It might be slowly, but broke is broke, no matter how slowly you get there.

5. WILL YOU HAVE THE FINANCIAL AND EMOTIONAL STAYING POWER TO SURVIVE THE LEARNING CURVE?

- Calculate your startup costs.

- Calculate your weekly cost of operations, including payroll. For payroll, don't forget to consider the statutory benefits employers are required to pay on behalf of their employees.

- Calculate your monthly cost of operations, including occupancy, accounting, advertising, insurance, utilities, regulatory compliance, uniforms, etc.

- Realistically project your revenues, month by month, for the first two years. This is vital.

- Do the math. How much money will it take to keep this business happy, healthy, and strong until it becomes profitable? Can you afford to take this journey?

6. CALCULATE YOUR COST OF GROWTH

- Growth can be accomplished in five ways, but only three of these are in your direct control:

    * advertising

    * logo-wrapped vehicles, and

    * signage on a high-visibility storefront.

For the purposes of budgeting, all your investments in search engine optimization (SEO), social media, email, website maintenance, and influencer partnerships will be considered **advertising**, the same as TV, radio, outdoor, newspaper, magazines, and direct mail.

- The two forms of exposure that are not within your direct control are:

    * word of mouth

    * public relations

Advertising is what you buy from the sales department of the media. Public relations (PR) is what you get for free from journalists—the content creators of the media. Traditionally, in that simplest-of-all retail business with a 50 percent gross margin and a 2x inventory turn, the occupancy budget (rent) will be between 5 percent and 6 percent of sales, and the ad budget will be between 5 percent and 6 percent of sales. This would make your total **cost of exposure** (rent plus marketing) between 10 percent and 12 percent of sales. Obviously, the more you save on rent, the more you can spend on marketing.

But when you study the category leaders in most categories, you'll find that their cost of exposure is often 15 percent to 18 percent. It is a lot more expensive to "get the word out" than you probably expected.

7. GETTING STARTED

- Choose a name

    * Be careful that it isn't too generic, or you
      will blur yourself into your category. "The
      Plumbing Place" is a generic descriptive.

    * Be careful that it isn't too obscure or
      people will simply be confused. What does
      "The Blue Spot" sell?

- Create an entity

    * Will you be a C-corp, an S-corp, an LLC,
      a limited partnership, or something else?
      Every structure has its advantages and
      disadvantages. You will need an attorney
      and a CPA. When your business has a tax
      ID number, you can open a business bank
      account. You may also need to get a sales
      tax permit from your state.

- Choose where your business will be located

    * Do you need retail space, warehouse space,
      or both?

- Create an identity, a personality, for your business.

* You will need a look, a feel, a logo, and a series of signature phrases that no one uses except you.

* Don't assume that you can do this yourself. Talented designers and other marketing help are worth every penny you pay for them.

* Tell the marketplace that you exist. A website is essential, regardless of your business category, but you are going to need to do a lot more advertising and marketing than just the creation of a website. Who is going to do this for you? This is an extremely important decision. People can't buy from you if they haven't heard about you, and the cost of telling them about you might be much higher than you think.

* Will your business need company vehicles? If so, will they be wrapped with your logo and contact info?

8. CALCULATE YOUR RECURRING EXPENSES

These include occupancy, advertising, payroll, taxes, insurance, accounting, utilities, gasoline, maintenance for company vehicles (if any), and credit card fees (a percentage of your sales paid to the credit card companies for all the payments made to you by customers using credit cards).

Oh, and one super important thing. You're going to have to have some money to live on. In 1997, I worried constantly that I couldn't make payroll—I'd even keep my own paychecks aside because cash was so tight. Do yourself a favor and calculate what you need to sell each month to make a profit *and* pay yourself.

9. AVOID THESE COMMON CAUSES OF FAILURE

"Cash is tight, so I'll pay these taxes later."

If you don't stay on top of your sales taxes, payroll taxes, and income taxes, they will bring you down. It is extremely common for a new business owner to get to the end of the year and then say to their CPA, "How can I owe this much in taxes? I reinvested every penny back into the business."

Your CPA will then say, "Yes, but in the eyes of the government, you made a lot of profit and then invested that profit into assets that continue to have value. You bought computers, phones, trucks, and office furniture, all of which have an ongoing value. The government will let you deduct a certain amount immediately, but everything above that amount has to be deducted over time according to a 'depreciation schedule' based on the life expectancy of what you purchased."

You're sitting there looking at a near-empty bank account while your CPA is telling you, "Congratulations! You had a really good year! Above and beyond all the sales taxes, payroll withholding taxes, and estimated quarterly income taxes you've already paid, you need to pay another $80,000 immediately, or you're going to get hit with penalties and interest. Again, congratulations on a great year!"

"Cash is tight, so I'll cut back on my advertising."

This seems like a good idea at first, because your costs will decline more quickly than your sales. But like everything else that has weight and speed, ad campaigns are painfully slow to get rolling, and you can also coast for a while before you realize that your flywheel is losing momentum.

When you quit advertising, you put yourself into a position where competitors can come from behind and leapfrog over you. Keep this in mind because it works both ways. When your competitors decide to save money by not advertising, they put themselves into position for you to come from behind and leapfrog them as well.

Know the difference between making money, cash in the bank, and growing the value of your business.

Your accountant might look at your bank statements and say you're not making any money, but remember, you're investing in your business so it can grow in value.

And speaking of being financially aware, one-third of all small business bankruptcies each year are the direct result of embezzlement. It sounds crazy, but you probably even know someone who's been the victim of embezzlement, they just don't talk about it.

As an owner, it's important to build a system to safeguard yourself. When it's time to grow, and you are no longer writing and signing all the checks yourself, make sure the person who writes the checks isn't the one who signs them, and vice versa. This can remove the most basic temptation: writing a check to yourself.

Don't miss a pivot.

Kodak dominated the photography industry for decades. Their research labs even invented filmless photography. But in the 1980s, leadership failed to recognize just how disruptive digital photography would be, choosing to stick close to their "core" businesses in film and photographic chemicals. Toys"R"Us faced a similar demise when it failed to adapt to changing consumer behavior and ramp up its online presence.

Even the most established businesses can fail when they get stuck in the status quo. Listen to your customers, anticipate their needs, and don't be afraid of change.

28

PANIC CAN BE
YOUR FRIEND

FAR TOO OFTEN, INTELLIGENT PEOPLE OVERTHINK
their plans when they should have trusted their instincts.

Theodor Geisel was at sea aboard the *MS Kungsholm*
when a storm hit and it appeared as though the ship
might sink. To distract himself as he was trying to stay
calm below deck, Theodor focused his mind on the sound
of the ship's engine,

*pum-pum-**PUM**-pum-pum-**PUM**-pum-pum-**PUM**-
pum-pum-**PUM**-pum-pum-**PUM**-pum-pum-**PUM**-
pum-pum-**PUM***

and began making up a little story whose syllables matched the odd rhythm of that machine.

The storm passed, but Theodor continued writing until he finished the story's final lines:

And that is a story that no one can beat

And to think that I saw it on Mulberry Street.

The following year, Theodor Geisel gave himself an honorary doctorate and published his first book, *And to Think That I Saw it on Mulberry Street,* under his middle name, Seuss. You've heard of Dr. Seuss, right?

He harnessed his panic, unleashing the signature rhyming style that would go on to make him famous.

Here's another example when time pressure and panic gave birth to great inspiration and focus. Ted Leonsis was on a little commuter airplane that lost the ability to use its wing flaps and landing gear. Face-to-face with the possibility of impending death, Ted wrote a list of 101 things he promised himself he would do if he lived. That list took twenty minutes, just enough time to safely land.

By May 27, 2021, Ted had accomplished eighty-one of those things.

> « What would be on your list of 101 things to do before you die? »

I was at MIT listening to a lecture when I heard Ted's story and was given an assignment to write down 101 things. Now!

What I wrote on my list is unimportant. And what Ted wrote on his list is unimportant.

What is important is what you write on your list.

You've got twenty minutes. Start a timer. Start your list. Let panic be your friend.

Don't overthink it. Don't worry about spelling or grammar.

If you live, you can correct those things later.

Your ship is sinking. Your plane is falling from the sky.

If you're going to finish your list, you have to add something every twelve seconds.

Start your twenty-minute timer.

Go.

29

DON'T READ THIS CHAPTER UNTIL YOU'VE DONE YOUR 101

It's important that you write your 101 life goals under extreme time pressure. Otherwise you'll overthink it and write down what you think you *ought* to want instead of what you really want.

Mark Twain said 150 years ago, "I can teach anybody how to get what they want out of life. The problem is that I can't find anybody who can tell me what they want."

Did you do it? Did you write your 101 life goals in twenty minutes?

Congratulations! Now you know what's really important to you. You know what you want. You know what you value. You know what you **believe**. And that's a much bigger deal than you think.

When Simon Sinek flew from New York to visit us, Cameron Herold and I had lunch with him. While we were waiting for our food, he showed us something that looked like an upside-down ice cream cone with "Vision" at the top.

Simon now had my undivided attention, because I already knew that good things always start with a sharp, bright **vision** of the future that trickles down into the rest of your business.

A couple of years later, when Cameron and I heard Simon's TED Talk, we looked at each other, smiled, and simultaneously said, "He finally perfected his Big Idea."

I think a lot of people misunderstand what Simon was telling us in that famous seventeen-minute, fifty-two-second TED Talk. They seem to think that "Start with Why" is just a new way of finding your Unique Selling Proposition, but I don't believe that's what Simon was trying to tell us at all.

When he approaches the two-minute mark of that famous TED Talk in Puget Sound, he says,

> As it turns out, all the great inspiring leaders and organizations in the world, whether it's Apple or Martin Luther King or the Wright brothers, they all think, act, and communicate the exact same way. And it's the complete opposite to everyone else. All I did was codify it, and it's probably the world's simplest idea. I call it **The Golden Circle**.

Even though Simon uses the word "why" twenty-eight times in that talk, did you realize that he uses the word "**believe**" thirty-two times, and twenty-eight of those thirty-two times are in his most high-impact statements?

At four minutes:

> Here's how Apple actually communicates: "Everything we do, we **believe** in challenging the status quo. We **believe** in thinking differently."

At five and a half minutes:

> People don't buy what you do; they buy why you do it. The goal is not to do business with everybody who

needs what you have. The goal is to do business with people who **believe** what you **believe**.

At seven and a half minutes:

The goal is not just to sell to people who need what you have; the goal is to sell to people who **believe** what you **believe**. The goal is not just to hire people who need a job, it's to hire people who **believe** what you **believe**. I always say that, you know, if you hire people just because they can do a job, they'll work for your money, but if they **believe** what you **believe**, they'll work for you with blood and sweat and tears.

At nine and a half minutes, after talking about the failure of Samuel Pierpont Langley, Simon says,

The difference was, Orville and Wilbur were driven by a cause, by a purpose, by a belief. They **believed** that if they could figure out this flying machine, it'll change the course of the world. Samuel Pierpont Langley was different. He wanted to be rich and he wanted to be famous. He was in pursuit of the result. He was in pursuit of the riches. And lo and behold, look what happened. The people who **believed** in the Wright brothers' dream worked with them with blood and sweat and tears.

And just as Simon approaches the eleven-minute mark, he says,

> People don't buy what you do; they buy why you do it. If you talk about what you **believe**, you will attract those who **believe** what you **believe**. But why is it important to attract those who **believe** what you **believe**?

About thirteen minutes in, Simon gets his airplane lined up with the runway. He's ready to land this thing.

> People don't buy what you do; they buy why you do it and what you do simply proves what you **believe**. In fact, people will do the things that prove what they **believe**. The reason that person bought the iPhone in the first six hours, stood in line for six hours, was because of what they **believed** about the world, and how they wanted everybody to see them.

Just before the fifteen-minute mark, Simon makes his point again.

> People don't buy what you do; they buy why you do it, and what you do simply serves as the proof of what you **believe**.

And at fifteen and a half minutes, his airplane wheels touch the tarmac when he starts talking about Martin Luther King Jr.

He wasn't the only man in America who suffered in a pre–civil rights America. In fact, some of his ideas were bad. But he had a gift. He didn't go around telling people what needed to change in America. He went around and told people what he **believed**. "I **believe**, I **believe**, I **believe**," he told people. And people who **believed** what he **believed** took his cause, and they made it their own, and they told people. And some of those people created structures to get the word out to even more people. And lo and behold, 250,000 people showed up on the right day at the right time to hear him speak.

How many of them showed up for him? Zero. They showed up for themselves. It's what they **believed** about America that got them to travel in a bus for eight hours to stand in the sun in Washington in the middle of August. It's what they **believed**, and it wasn't about black versus white: 25 percent of the audience was white.

Dr. King **believed** that there are two types of laws in this world: those that are made by a higher authority and those that are made by men. And not until all the laws that are made by men are consistent with the laws made by the higher authority will we live in a just world. It just so happened that the Civil Rights Movement was the perfect thing to help him bring his cause to life. We followed, not for him, but for ourselves. By the way, he gave the "I Have a Dream" speech, not the "I Have a Plan" speech.

« When you listed your 101 life goals in twenty minutes, you were listing your values. You were listing the things you believe in.

You believe, you believe, you believe… »

I applaud you. And in my mind, I see Mark Twain, Dr. Seuss, Ted Leonsis, and Simon Sinek applauding you, as well.

30

DO YOU WANT TO BE KING OR DO YOU WANT TO BE RICH?

EVERY BUSINESS OWNER IS THE KING OF THEIR OWN little kingdom.

Joe answers the phone, "Joe's Radiator Repair Service, Joe speaking."

No one can tell Joe what to do. It's good to be king.

But when "king" and "rich" come into conflict, do you want to be king, or do you want to be rich?

I came across this quote from Michael Gerber: "If your business depends on you, you don't own a business. You have a job and it's the worst job in the world because you're working for a lunatic."

> « When you work for yourself, you're controlled by the work you're required to do. But when you own a business where other people do the work you're selling, you have freedom. »

That is why most business owners plateau. When your talent, experience, and dedication have not been successfully transferred to others, you hit a ceiling that lets you see more customers out there, but you can't climb high enough to get to them.

This is the founder's dilemma. You become rich only when you have the freedom to quit working *in* the business and start working *on* the business. And I don't mean rich only in terms of freedom and money, but also rich in terms of learning and opportunity.

When you are finally ready to free yourself from working in the business, and you are prepared to start working on it, you have to add people to your team who are extremely good at doing the things you hate to do.

I'm not good at recruiting people, and I don't like managing them, either. And the discipline of weekly check-ins is not something I've ever been able to master. I'm good at seeing opportunities and dreaming up big ideas, so I needed someone who is a master of operational excellence.

Our COO, Erik Church, had a wide variety of different experiences, including a career in the military, before he pivoted to running a business. He's incredibly good at doing all the things I don't like; he's the yin to my yang. By combining our strengths and fostering an extremely passionate team, we've gone from $100 million to $500 million in record time, and $1 billion is clearly in our crosshairs.

《 Take a moment to look at your business and ask, "What am I doing, or not doing, that is keeping my business at its current level? Do I have the people I need at my side? 》

The first challenge you will face is building your business to $1 million a year. At a million dollars, you will have achieved your most difficult milestone and a degree of success. That's when you face the founder's dilemma: "No one can run this business as well as I do. No one can answer the phones as well as I do. No one can pitch the press as well as I do."

As long as you continue to believe that, you will remain the hardworking king of a little, one-million-dollar kingdom. But sooner or later a competitor will come to your town who doesn't have those self-limiting beliefs. That competitor will advertise aggressively, hire people enthusiastically, and gain momentum until the truth finally smacks you in the face: you built a sandcastle on the beach and now the tide is rolling in.

Bestselling author Noam Wasserman wrote a case study on my original company, The Rubbish Boys, in *Harvard Business Review*. That case study was about the founder's dilemma; that fork in the road where every entrepreneur has to decide what truly motivates them. Do they want to be king, or do they want to be rich?

Noam Wasserman saw me as a prime example of someone who wanted to be king. I read his article, saw the truth in it, and decided I would rather be rich.

> You become rich when you realize that you are in the people business and that your job is to hire, train, and empower people who will make your customers happy. You become rich when you realize that it takes a village to run a business. You need a culture that embraces people with complementary skills so that you can achieve size, scope, and impact.

Getting to $1 million a year is hard because you have so few people in your business with you. As the founder, you will have to wear several hats and do several jobs. Every day is a grind, but you know that getting to $5 million is easy. All you have to do is get out of your own way, turn those important jobs over to other people, and start working *on* your business rather than *in* it.

31

BIGGER AND BETTER TOGETHER

WHEN YOU'RE SURROUNDED BY PASSIONATE PEOPLE, you'll share brilliant ideas. When you have a team that comes together to cheer each other on, there's nothing you can't accomplish. But the best part of building something bigger and better together is that it's FUN.

If you want people to follow your vision so you can begin building something bigger and better together, you have to capture their hearts and minds. One way we do this is through our 101 Life Goals program. It's how we show our team that we're interested in their lives, we care, and that we support them.

Our objective is to inspire our people to imagine big possibilities for themselves. We love asking our franchise partners and team members to write down 101 Life Goals. Then we become their cheerleaders, encouraging them, supporting them, and giving them whatever they need to build the life of their dreams.

You would be surprised at the number of things on those lists that you can easily help to make happen.

One of Erik Church's life goals was to experience the Calgary Stampede with his daughter.

Tanya Hall wanted to read *Anna Karenina* in Russian. When I asked her about it, she said, "My dad was Russian and he said to me on his deathbed, 'Honey, go read *Anna Karenina*.'" I still remember the tears streaming down her cheeks when we did just a little bit to help make that possible.

Earl Sotto wanted to sit with his wife on the *Friends* couch where the show was filmed at Warner Bros. Studios. I smile every time I look at that photo.

Kerrie Shakespeare wanted to drive a race car.

Lara Gribben wanted to ride a motorbike through Vietnam.

Phil Bubis wanted to feast with his coworkers on a roast pig.

Alannah Niven wanted to meet Halsey.

Vaughn Joyce wanted to help release baby sea turtles back into the ocean.

Rachel Stout wanted to learn to change the oil on her motorcycle.

Ryan Anderson wanted to throw the opening pitch at a professional baseball game.

Sarah Robinson wanted to eat at Pujol, one of the best restaurants in the world.

Greg Brown wanted to learn traditional blacksmithing methods.

Jenna Sadko wanted to hold a bird of prey.

Yvonne Munro wanted to reunite her seven siblings.

Jordan Tait wanted to swim in a glacier lagoon.

Romi Weiss wanted to attend Comic-Con.

Marc Asgeirson wanted to visit the birthplace of his grandfather.

Shelley Adam wanted to learn to drive a big rig.

Matt Atack wanted to see an alligator from an airboat.

It doesn't matter why these people wanted to do these things. What matters is that someone cared about what they wanted and helped make one of those things happen.

You can't take care of your customers without taking care of your team first. And taking care of your team is *fun*. We've already published a private edition of a big, beautiful, full-color coffee-table book that celebrates 101 of our people as each of them experienced one of the goals on their list, and we plan to publish more books like it.

I believe my most important job as CEO is to share my vision with my team and make sure they see themselves in that vision. I'm not saying, "Hey, as an entrepreneur, here's what I want to do, *rah-rah-rah*."

I'm talking about something bigger than that. I'm talking about encouraging big dreams and the living of big lives while celebrating the uniqueness of our personal goals, always remembering that we are bigger and better TOGETHER.

Will you join me? All you have to do is figure out how to say, "I see you. I hear you."

If we do it right, the impact of this will continue long beyond your lifetime and mine.

And that's a pretty special thing.

32

WHAT A LITTLE COMPANY IN DENMARK TAUGHT US

IN 2020, CHICK-FIL-A GENERATED $13.7 BILLION IN sales to become the third most successful restaurant chain behind Starbucks at number two and McDonald's at number one.

The McDonald's franchise launched in 1955.

Starbucks only had four locations in the early 1980s, which were all in Seattle.

Chick-fil-A took off in 1967. Their original name was Dwarf House and they sold steaks and burgers. I'd say Plan B worked really well for them, wouldn't you?

Chick-fil-A gets more than 20,000 franchisee applications a year and chooses only seventy-five to eighty, according to *Business Insider*. That means you have a 0.4 percent chance of becoming a Chick-fil-A franchisee.

Have you ever eaten at Panda Express? They opened their second location in 1985. Today they have 2,200 locations doing more than $3 billion a year.

McDonald's, Starbucks, Chick-fil-A, Panda Express, 1-800-GOT-JUNK?, WOW 1 DAY PAINTING, Shack Shine, and every other successful franchise is just a different manifestation of what every child learns from assembling a LEGO project:

1. Look at the picture on the box. This is what it should look like when you're done. Everything you need to create this picture is inside that box. (Are you beginning to understand the importance of the Painted Picture we talked about earlier?)

2. Follow the illustrated instructions, picture by picture, and your project will turn

out perfectly, even if you're building the
new *Star Wars* Millennium Falcon kit
containing 7,541 pieces.

Worldwide LEGO sales in 2020 were about $7 billion.
Not bad for a little company in Denmark, right?

Question: How big do you think LEGO would be today if
they sold big buckets of blocks with no pictures and no
instructions and told people, "You can make whatever
you want from them! Just imagine what you want, and
then make it!"

Now you know why nine out of ten new businesses that
succeed are franchises.

All you have to do is follow the instructions.

33

HOW TO CHOOSE
THE FRANCHISE
THAT'S RIGHT
FOR YOU

AT THE FIRST HINT OF FALL, OUR 1-800-GOT-JUNK? franchise partners transition from their branded polos to their fleece vests. WOW 1 DAY PAINTING franchise owners Brent, Simon, Chris, and Hugh have invested in a fleet of twenty-seven wrapped vehicles. There are so many on the road now that people in Toronto come up to them and say, "I see your brand *everywhere*." And it's hard to find me without my branded Chucks on.

When you find the right franchise, you won't be able to stop from loudly and proudly sharing it with the world. And your community of like-minded people will help spur you on.

These questions will help you find the right franchise system for you.

1. "Is this something I can see myself doing? Is this a business I feel good about?"

I'm not saying, "Follow your passion." People who follow their passion usually fail because they're trying to turn their hobby into a business. I'm saying that you need to feel good about what you do each day.

2. Is this franchise the leader in its category?

The low-cost provider cannot provide an exceptional customer experience. But there are plenty of companies that do it a little bit worse and sell it a little bit cheaper. These companies always attract customers who never feel like they got their money's worth.

When customers say, "They're expensive but I love them!" they are talking about the category leader.

> Some people have more time than money.
>
> Some people have more money than time.
>
> Which customer do you want to sell to?

3. What does the research say?

Find customer reviews about the service or product. Go beyond that and find out what the franchisees say about their own business—do they love it? Learn as much as you can about the culture and ask yourself if you'll thrive in the system, and if these people will help make you a better business owner. Research: find out how often the franchise has been sued by a franchise partner and how many franchise partners are trying to sell their business. If you can find a few for sale, that's not a good sign.

When someone contemplates marriage, their friends ask, "Have you spent any time with the family? Because you're marrying the whole family!" Becoming a franchise partner is like that. You're marrying into a family, so make sure it's one you like.

4. How good is the marketing provided by the franchise?

If a franchise allows you to create your own ads, you're looking at an extremely weak franchise. Homemade ads created by franchise partners create an inconsistent public image. Where nonstandard advertising is acceptable, you can be sure that performance standards are nonexistent as well. Turnkey marketing plans are one of the marks of a strong franchise.

5. What are the royalties?

In a franchise system, you get what you pay for. Don't be scared off by high royalties—those are an indication that you'll get more coaching and support, and that the company is financially secure. A franchise that charges suspiciously low royalties likely won't have much to offer you.

6. How likely are my customers to become repeat customers?

Selling a first-time customer is expensive because it requires a lot of advertising. But selling that same customer a second, third, fourth, and fiftieth time is easy if they had a good experience the first time. If you want to own a business with repeat customers who will recommend you to their friends, you need to own a franchise that provides detailed training and has high performance standards.

7. Is this a service or product that makes people feel good?

It's always easier and more fun to sell things that make people smile. When the customer is always happy to see you, you're in a great business.

34

IDENTITY, PURPOSE, AND ADVENTURE

Nando Parrado was on a plane that crashed in the Andes Mountains at 12,000 feet above sea level. Twelve of the airplane's forty-five passengers were killed. When the remaining thirty-three passengers emerged from the wreckage, they stepped onto an ocean of ice, snow, and black rock. The temperature was thirty-five degrees below zero and no one was dressed for it. Five more people died that night.

Then an avalanche a few days later reduced their original tribe of forty-five to just sixteen people.

Believing they were six kilometers from the nearest town, Nando and his friend Roberto decided to go get help. "If we can climb over the summit of that mountain to the west, we will see the green valleys of Chile beyond." But when they finally made it to the top of that mountain, they were looking down into another valley with another mountain peak beyond it.

Business is a lot like that. You see an obstacle and think, "As soon as I get beyond that, I'm home free." But when that obstacle is behind you, a new and different one takes its place.

When Nando Parrado speaks of the seventy-two days it took them to traverse seventy kilometers through the Andes Mountains, he sounds like an entrepreneur. He speaks of critical decision-making, innovative improvisation, and committed teamwork. But he also stresses the importance of singular commitment, saying, "I firmly believe there comes a time for individuality."

If you are going to own a business, you need to get used to the idea that there will always be another problem to solve and another frozen mountain to climb.

Life is about three things:

1. Identity: "Who am I?"

2. Purpose: "Why am I here?"

3. Adventure: "What must I overcome?"

> Owning a business gives you a focused purpose and a never-ending adventure.
>
> When you are safe at home, you wish you were having an adventure. And when you are having an adventure, you wish you were safe at home.

Are you sure you are ready for adventure?

35

FOCUS, FAITH, AND EFFORT

《 Building a business is like building a rocket ship while you're flying it.

To succeed, you're going to need Focus, Faith, and Effort.

If you fail, it will be because you didn't Focus, you didn't have Faith, or you didn't put in the Effort.

It's just that simple. 》

FOCUS

A laser beam is a light so intensely focused you can cut through steel with it.

My first experience with focus was back during my Rubbish Boys days before we became 1-800-GOT-JUNK?. Realizing that I was spread too thin, I decided to cut metropolitan Vancouver in half at Knight Street. "I'm just not crossing Knight Street, even if you're just one block beyond it. I am focused and I'm staying in my area."

Focusing more energy into a smaller area was extremely beneficial to my business.

Focusing your energy will be extremely beneficial to you, too.

FAITH

You've got to have faith in the system, have faith in the processes, and have faith in your team.

A franchise partner named Alan Remer called one day and said, "Brian, I hate my team."

I said, "Alan, I'll bet they hate you, too."

He said, "It's just not working. I don't have the right people. Their attitude stinks."

I told him about firing all eleven of my team members in 1994. I wrapped it up by saying, "Alan, I confessed the truth to all eleven of those people. I told them that I had failed them as their coach, and that I hadn't encouraged them properly. I took responsibility for their failure." My goal in telling that story was to show Alan that he shared some responsibility for their bad attitude and their failure. I was trying to tell him to stick with his people, have faith in them, coach them, and turn them around.

Alan called me a few days later and said, "I did it."

"Did what?"

"I fired my whole team."

Alan understood he needed to have faith in his team and decided to start over again with a clean slate. It turned out to be the right decision. Alan is doing fantastic today.

Another franchise partner, Finton, was a person I really liked, but his franchise just wasn't working. So I got on a plane and flew to his city.

The first thing I did was track down each of his trucks. 1-800-GOT-JUNK? is all about "clean, shiny trucks and happy, uniformed drivers," remember? The first truck I encountered had been in an accident and had a big dent in the front. It was rusty and looked terrible. Worst of all, the J was missing off his 1-800-GOT-JUNK? phone number.

"1-800-GOT-UNK?"

I called Finton and asked if he could meet me for a beer.

When I asked him to help me understand his struggles, he blamed everything except his own lack of Focus, Faith, and Effort. "This city is unlike any other city. Everyone here owns a pickup truck. And the economy sucks. And it snows half the year."

Finally, I said, "Finton, I don't think this is for you. I don't think you have faith in our brand. I don't think you have faith in yourself and in your ability to build this. I don't think you have faith in your city."

Finton was the first franchise partner I ever booted out of the system. But he understood what I was saying, and he agreed with me. Three months later, Dave Harrop bought the business and quickly made it the third-highest-volume franchise in our system, which at the time had fifty franchise partners.

The pickup trucks owned by the citizens of that city, the sluggish economy, and the snow didn't seem to be a problem for Dave, who came to the table with faith in himself, his team, the system, and the brand.

EFFORT

There is no substitute for hard work. We get a lot of franchise inquiries from people who want to play "businessperson." They have no interest in pounding the pavement, finding employees, making sales, and working hard. They want to sit behind a desk.

Here's the bottom line. You have to score nine out of ten on Focus, nine out of ten on Faith, nine out of ten on Effort. Do that and you will succeed every time. Every time a person scores low in one of those three areas, they fail. It's just that simple.

Focus, Faith, and Effort shine so brightly that customers can see them sparkling.

THIS STORY MAKES ME FEEL REALLY PROUD

Our newest franchise, Shack Shine, offers gutter cleaning as one of the services to make your home Twinkle, Sparkle, and Glow. Recently, we got a call from a Shack Shine customer who asked us to send a van with a two-story ladder to her home. She had locked her keys in her house and felt certain that an upstairs window was unlocked. "I just need you to crawl in that window and unlock the front door for me. I'm happy to pay."

We're always happy to help.

When the Shack Shine team member unlocked the door for her, he asked, "Why didn't you call a locksmith?"

She answered with a smile, "I'm not certain I trust a locksmith, but I am certain that I trust you."

Like I was saying: Focus, Faith, and Effort shine so brightly that customers can see them sparkling.

36

LET'S TALK A LITTLE BIT MORE ABOUT FOCUS, FAITH, AND EFFORT

THE YEAR IS 1918. CHARLES M. SCHWAB IS THE PRESIDENT of a small steel company. He arranges a meeting with Ivy Lee, a productivity consultant.

On the appointed day, Lee outlined his firm's services and promised, "With our service, you'll know how to manage your people more effectively."

Schwab said, "We don't need more *knowing*. We need more *doing*. We've already got the knowledge. What we need is action. Give me something that will get people to do *what they already know how to do,* and I'll pay you anything you ask."

Lee said, "Do you have a sheet of paper?"

Schwab produced one.

Lee said, "Write down the **five most important things** you need to do tomorrow."

Schwab wrote down the five things. Lee didn't even look at them. He said, "Tomorrow morning, look at item one and start working on it. Look at it every fifteen minutes until item one is completed. Then tackle item two. If it takes you all day to complete item one, at least you will be working on the most important thing you need to do that day. If you cannot finish all five in one day using this method, you could not have finished them by any other method, either."

Lee shook Schwab's hand and said, "Do it for ninety days. If you see a lift in productivity, write me a check for what you think it was worth." And then he walked away.

Ninety days later, Schwab mailed Lee a check for $25,000—about $400,000 by today's standards—with a note saying, "Your method is exactly what I was looking for."

Lee's method gave Schwab **focus.**

Schwab had **faith** the idea would work.

And his **effort** was energized by the miracle of the **flywheel**.

By looking at his Top Five every fifteen minutes, his efforts no longer added up, they multiplied.

Remember this example?

$1 + 2 + 3 + 4 + 5 = $ **15**

But...

$1 \times 2 \times 3 \times 4 \times 5 = $ **120**

$\times 1 \times 2 \times 3 \times 4 \times 5 = $ **14,400**

$\times 1 \times 2 \times 3 \times 4 \times 5 = $ **1,728,000**

$\times 1 \times 2 \times 3 \times 4 \times 5 = $ **207,360,000**

$\times 1 \times 2 \times 3 \times 4 \times 5 = $ **24,883,200,000**

Five years later, Schwab's little Bethlehem Steel Company was the biggest independent steel producer in the world and Charles M. Schwab was one of the richest men in America.

Do you have a sheet of paper?

What are five things that will move you from thinking about pursuing your dreams, into action?

What are the five most important things you need to do tomorrow?

Write them down.

37

YOUR CHAPTER

WELL, THIS IS IT, THE END OF OUR 90 MINUTES TOGETHER.

When we started this party back on page one, my goal was to encourage you, to help you move from dreaming to doing.

I've presented you with two equally awesome choices for starting your own business. What you do next is up to you. This is the start of your chapter.

So—are you ready to take action? Are you ready to start your own business? Will you choose to start from scratch or with a proven plan?

If you'd like to share your decision with a friend, send me a message on Instagram @brianscudamore. I'd love to support you as you BYOB!

APPENDICES

WORKSHEET 1: FIND YOUR PASSION, BUILD YOUR TEAM

Pulling out that sheet of paper and being honest about my strengths and weaknesses was an invaluable exercise. It gave me a chance to focus on what I love and do best, and it enabled me to build my team and business.

Now it's your turn.

1. Get out a sheet of paper.

2. Draw a line down the middle.

3. Label one side "Things I love/I'm good at/ don't want to let go of."

4. Label the other side "Things I don't like/I'm bad at/should let go of."

5. Be honest. Write everything down.

6. From this exercise, you will be able to create an understanding of what you should be doing, and what you should find an expert to do for you.

Things I love | Things I don't

WORKSHEET 2: YOUR TOP FIVE LIST

What are five things that will move you from **thinking** about pursuing your dreams, into **action**?

What are the five most important things you need to do tomorrow?

Write them down.

5 things keeping me from turning
my dreams into actions

1.

2.

3.

4.

5.

5 things I need to do tomorrow

1.

2.

3.

4.

5.

READING RECOMMENDATIONS: VISION

- *Start with Why*—Simon Sinek

- *Good to Great*—Jim Collins

- *Get a Grip*—Gino Wickman and Mike Paton

READING RECOMMENDATIONS: PEOPLE

- *The Culture Code*—Daniel Coyle

- *No Rules Rules: Netflix and the Culture of Reinvention*—Reed Hastings and Erin Meyer

- *Drive: The Surprising Truth about What Motivates Us*—Daniel H. Pink

- *Tribes*—Seth Godin

- *Dare to Lead*—Brené Brown

- *Elevate: Push beyond Your Limits and Unlock Success in Yourself and Others*—Bob Glazer

- *The Five Dysfunctions of a Team*—Patrick Lencioni

READING RECOMMENDATIONS: SYSTEMS

- *The E-Myth Revisited*—Michael Gerber

- *Scaling Up*—Verne Harnish

- *The Great Game of Business*—Jack Stack

WTF?! (Willing to Fail):
How Failure Can Be Your Key to Success

Read the Amazon bestseller
by Brian Scudamore

Entrepreneurship is a roller coaster of trial and error, laughter and tears, confusion and triumph. In WTF?! (Willing to Fail), serial entrepreneur Brian Scudamore takes you on an adventure that will convince you once and for all that you have exactly what it takes to succeed.

"It's not easy to turn one business into a multimillion-dollar success, and Brian Scudamore has done it four times. In his first book, he opens up about how he transformed a single junk truck into a home-services empire--and how if he can do it, anyone can."

—Robert Herjavec, celebrity entrepreneur on Shark Tank and
Dragon's Den and CEO of Herjavec Group

"Brian Scudamore is everyman's entrepreneur. This book tells the story of how everyone can, with great, productive joy, literally transform the world!"

—Michael E. Gerber, author of The E-Myth Books

"Brian Scudamore's story is both improbable and inspiring. 1-800-GOT-JUNK? is a story full of failure, struggle, crisis, and ultimately success through grit. Brian Scudamore is building billion-dollar brands with his own two hands."

—Guy Raz, host of NPR's How I Built This

For a free online version, please visit http://geni.us/wtfbook

WTF?! (Willing to Fail): How Failure Can
Be Your...

9 781544 527369